Essential
SELF-CARE

Essential
SELF-CARE

Tarot, breathwork, astrology, moon cycles,
restorative recipes, crystals, and more

Leah Vanderveldt

CICO BOOKS

Dedication: For Maeve & Fabian

This hardback edition published in 2025 by CICO Books
An imprint of Ryland Peters & Small Ltd
20–21 Jockey's Fields   1452 Davis Bugg Road
London WC1R 4BW   Warrenton, NC 27589
www.rylandpeters.com
Email: euregulations@rylandpeters.com

First published in 2020 as *Magical Self-care for Everyday Life*

10 9 8 7 6 5 4 3 2 1

Text © Leah Vanderveldt 2020, 2025
Design and photography © CICO Books 2020, 2025

A CIP record for this book is available from the British Library. US Library of Congress CIP data has been applied for.

ISBN: 978-1-80065-471-6

Printed in China

Photographer: Belle Daughtry
Designers: Eliana Holder and Alison Fenton
Editor: Dawn Bates
Commissioning editor: Kristine Pidkameny
Art director: Sally Powell
Head of production: Patricia Harrington
Publishing manager: Penny Craig
Publisher: Cindy Richards

The authorised representative in the EEA is
Authorised Rep Compliance Ltd.,
Ground Floor. 71 Lower Baggot Street,
Dublin, D01 P593, Ireland
www.arccompliance.com

Safety note: Please note that while the use of essential oils, herbs, incense, and particular practices refer to healing benefits, they are not intended to replace diagnosis of illness or ailments, or healing or medicine. Always consult your doctor or other health professional in the case of illness, pregnancy, and personal sensitivities and conditions. Neither the author nor the publisher can be held responsible for any claim arising out of the general information, recipes, and practices provided in the book.

For additional picture credits, see page 144.

MIX
Paper | Supporting responsible forestry
FSC® C106563
www.fsc.org

CONTENTS

Introduction

Self-care is the practice of treating yourself well. It can look different for everyone, but the heart of true self-care is knowing who you are and what you need, and honoring that while being kind to yourself.

The phrase "self-care" actually makes me a little uncomfortable. There's a certain air of privilege or woo-woo around the concept that a lot of people roll their eyes at. Some think they're too busy, tired, or low on funds to take part in it, but self-care belongs to everyone—and it's especially important if you feel stretched thin. Self-care is typically portrayed as the surface-level stuff that you can spend money on. There's nothing wrong with serums, massages, green smoothies, or whatever else you buy when you want a pick-me-up, but a lot of these things don't help us feel the way we want to feel at our core.

Real self-care is about what we do little by little every day to nourish our bodies, minds, and spirits so we can show up as the best version of ourselves. It's the practices, activities, and habits aimed at making us feel good at our core and bringing us back into balance. My foundational habits for self-care are: Hydration, eating well, getting enough sleep, practicing meditation daily, and connecting with others in-person. Boring, I know, but without these things, no other practice will be as potent.

The most important and hardest aspect of self-care is how we treat and speak to ourselves. I'm still nowhere near perfect at this, but over the past decade of my life, I've tried, studied, and grown to love a number of practices and tools, which are compiled for you within this book. These tools are the pillars of my self-care routines and rituals, since they help me ground my thoughts and come back to kindness. Hopefully this book can help you along your healing adventure and add a little more fun, kindness, and magic to the process.

The role of magic

To believe in magic is to choose to see the world around you in a certain light—one that helps, encourages, and supports you. If I have the choice between a daily grind with no common thread, bigger impact, or glimmer of mystery, or a life that feels synchronistic, connected, and playful, I will always choose the latter.

Magic invites us to entertain a change in perception and thought. Changing the way we talk to ourselves, the way we approach our needs, or how we interpret events can create shifts in our lives that sizzle with possibility—for our internal life and our communities. Magical living gives us an opportunity to claim our power, make the changes we seek, and create a life that lights us up. And the best part is, we already have everything we need within us at this very moment.

When we use rituals and tools that might be considered mystical, witchy, or esoteric to identify and address our needs, that is magical self-care. It requires being inquisitive, diving deep, and trusting yourself and your instincts. It's a process of self-care that combines the earthy and the spiritual for personal evolution and healing.

Magical self-care is about creating a better relationship with yourself through curiosity, awareness, and intention. It requires deep trust in yourself and discovering what's best for you on a holistic (physical + mental + emotional + spiritual) level. It's about unlocking your own personal brand of intuition and magic by getting you in touch with yourself, your worth, and your power. Before we get started, let's jump into some terms used throughout this book.

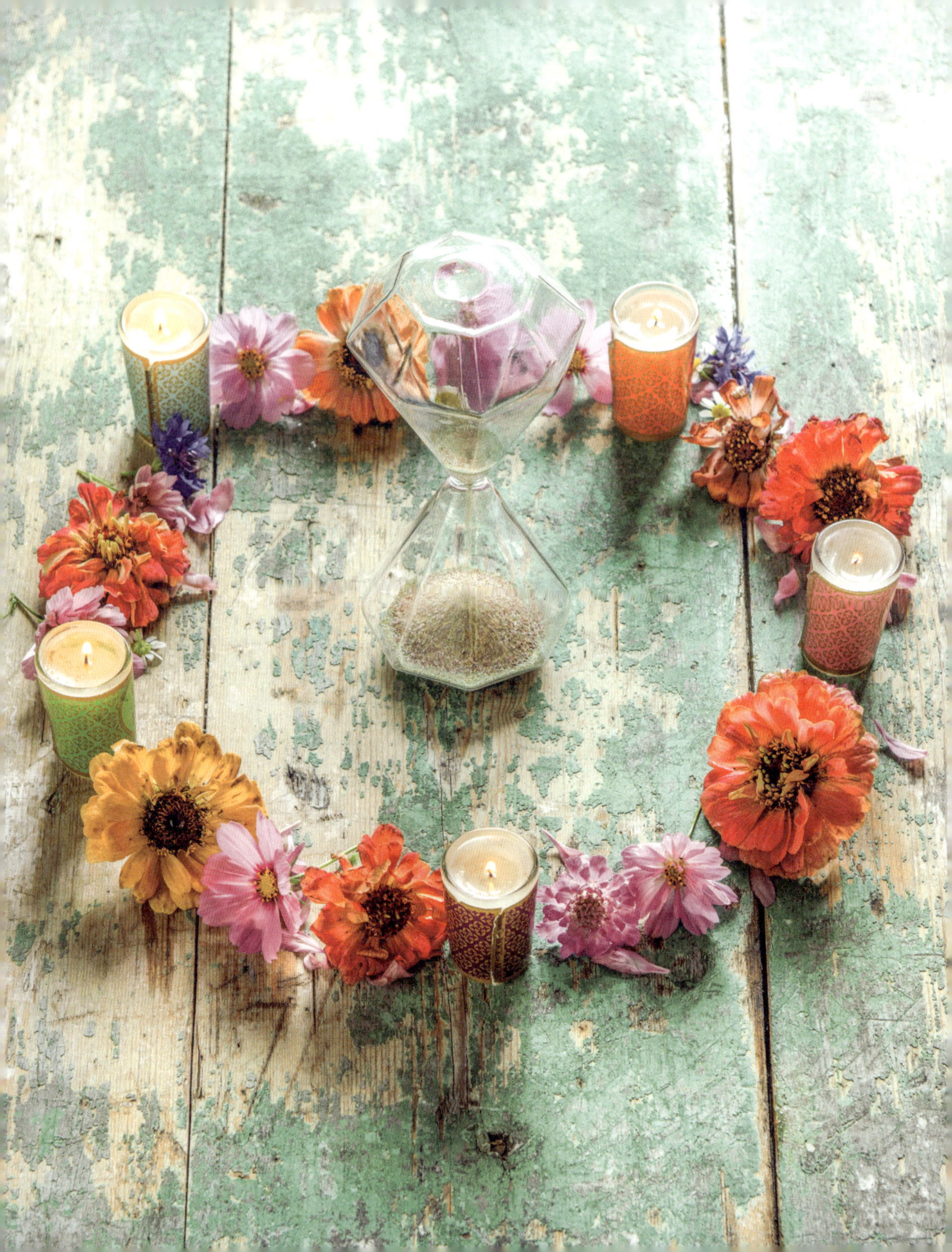

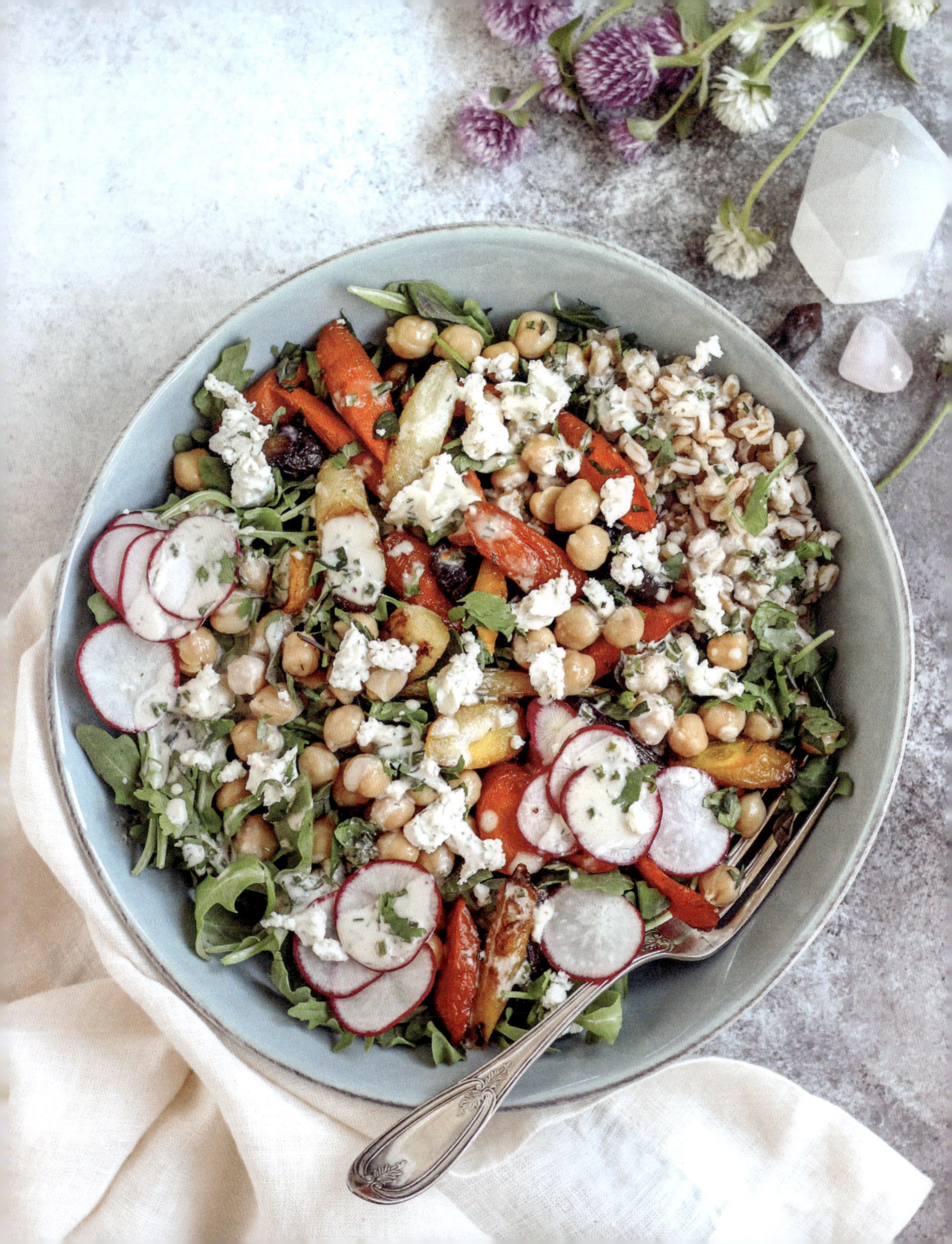

WITCHY

Witchy is a term for all things mystical, spiritual, and magical. While Wiccan and Pagan religions are very influential in many witchy rituals, you don't need to be a part of them to consider yourself a witch. Conversely, you can be a witch and adhere to any religious beliefs you want. Having a witchy and magical self-care practice is deeply individual and all about finding what resonates for you.

A witch is someone who recognizes their abilities and magic and uses them to create change in their life. They trust their own power and wisdom—especially if it's contrary to convention and the patriarchy—and they act on their intuition from a place of self-trust and trust in the universe.

THE UNIVERSE

When I say the universe in this book, I'm referring to a higher power that connects us to something bigger than ourselves. You can substitute it for Goddess, Love, Mother Earth, God, Divine, Spirit, Creator, Nature, or whatever strikes a chord with you.

CORE SELF

I refer to the core self throughout this book. It can also be called the true self, authentic self, highest self, or soul self. I like to think of it as the essence of who we are and who we were brought on this earth to be. It's like a pearl within the oyster—something beautiful and unique contained by our outer shell. Our outer shell protects the core, but this tough exterior is built up over time by outside influences and societal conditioning. The shell has a purpose but often prevents us from showing who we truly are to the world.

The more we can see glimpses of the core version of ourselves through intuitive and witchy practices, the more we can access it to share its wisdom, open-heartedness, and magic.

INTUITION

This is the "just feels right"/niggling sensation you get. Intuition is much quieter than your typical brain/ego voice that's loud, fear-based, and worried about what others might think. The ego isn't bad, but it's often misguided and programmed by things outside of us, so it doesn't always align with our core self. We want the two to work together with intuition in the management role, leading the way. The most important part is starting the conversation with our intuition.

Magical self-care encourages us to start asking, listening to, and following our intuition, and every modality—from Tarot to manifestation—is a different way to approach this wisdom within us. Let your intuition guide you throughout these pages, helping you choose and create the right rituals for you.

RITUAL

Rituals are activities with meaning and intention behind them. Different than a routine, these can be things we do regularly or once in a while for the purpose of leading us into a more present awareness. Through a small series of actions that make up a ritual, we can ground ourselves in the moment and connect to ourselves in a way that's enjoyable and purposeful.

I suggest plenty of rituals throughout each chapter, but I also walk you through creating your own ritual for each of the self-care tools. A ritual you conceive for yourself using your instincts is the most powerful because it comes from your wisdom and gifts (aka your magic). Building your own ritual is one of the best ways you can practice working with your creative magical energy, and it will help shape the unique way you'll work with these tools for your own self-care.

CULTURAL SENSITIVITY

An important aspect of using magical tools is awareness. I aim to be conscious when buying and using magical tools. If I use something outside of my cultural heritage, I research it and make sure I'm as respectful as possible. If you choose to use tools like

Palo Santo from South America or white sage from North America, be aware and respectful of the cultural backgrounds that these things come from and make sure they are responsibly sourced. We all deserve healing, but it's important not to take something from a heritage that isn't your own without honoring and acknowledging the history and significance that precedes you—especially if you're of white European descent. Be thoughtful about your choices and seek out tools that belong to your personal heritage, too.

SETTING INTENTIONS

Intention is everything. For the practices within these pages, as well as many things in life, having an intention or purpose behind what you're doing can help you get the most out of your experience. The point of an intention is to get to the heart of what you want and why.

A few questions to guide you to your intention could be: Why do I want to do x? How do I want to feel? What would help me feel that way? What am I trying to heal?

Different to goals, which often focus on getting something tangible, intentions are about having things feel a certain way. An intention is something that can anchor your practice or a cycle and help you remember your why. If you can get clear on your intention before creating a ritual, spell, or project of any kind, your experience will be richer and the result more powerful.

HEALING

Healing is a way of coming back to who we are at our core in an emotional and spiritual way. Healing is an ongoing process of learning to love all parts of ourselves and live in alignment with our core self. It can look like letting go of regret, resentment, or past hurt and welcoming in more love and acceptance of ourselves and others. Healing is a difficult process, full of contraction, expansion, heavy emotions, and realizations, but it's the single most rewarding gift we can give ourselves. We're all at various states of healing at all times, and may never be fully healed, but learning how to become consciously engaged in your own healing is when magic starts to happen.

How to use this book

Most of us don't have the time or the means for a complicated 2-hour morning routine that includes every crystal, tonic, and exercise. Instead, I offer these ideas to you in ways that are easy to include in your life and don't feel forced. They aim to be:

Quick: Most of these exercises and practices will require 30 minutes or less of your time and can be made shorter or longer depending on what you want. The Jump In sections are there to help you take action when you feel inspired to start using a modality in the moment.

Adaptable: If something doesn't work for you or feel quite right, skip it. The Create Your Own Ritual sections will encourage you to make it your own. Take what you like, and leave the rest. Learn as you go and don't take on too much at once.

Affordable: There will be some things that you might have to buy if you're interested in using them, like a Tarot deck, herbs for making infusions, or a candle here and there—but most items used in this book will be relatively inexpensive or free.

Think of the chapters and the practices within them like a menu for you to choose from in different seasons of your life and throughout the year. These methods and tools are intended to help you on your magical self-care journey, not to overwhelm you. There's no need to work through the book in order or do everything in it. There's likely one or two things that will really intrigue you—start there and keep an open mind to the rest.

A few other things I've included for each chapter:

RECIPES

Our intuition lives in our body, so when we hydrate and feed our bodies well, we nurture our intuition by extension. I've included wholesome, nourishing recipes in each chapter to ground magical rituals in something physical and to support our connection to our core self.

Our power is rooted in our sense of worthiness, and one way we can practice self-worth is to lovingly prepare meals for ourselves. Magical food is food made with intention that brings you joy and satisfaction. My hope is that you will cook things you love (whether that's my recipes or something else) as part of self-care.

TAROT REFLECTIONS

The three-card Tarot spreads included in each chapter serve as a point of reflection that can help us deepen our understanding of a subject or how we can work with it in a more personal way. Simply shuffle your deck and think of each question while you pull a card. Write down your responses and initial reactions to each card and how it relates to your question. Listen to and explore your intuitive responses. If Tarot isn't your thing, these questions can also be used as journaling prompts.

RESOURCES

This book is a jumping-off point to help you find and dive into the practices that are the most beneficial, healing, and magical for you. The resources section on pages 139–140 is full of teachers that I've learned from. It can help you learn more through books, online courses, podcasts, Instagram posts, newsletters, and more.

My intention for this book is that it supports and guides those interested in awakening to their power, cultivating a kinder relationship with themselves, and choosing to see their lives as successive moments of magic.

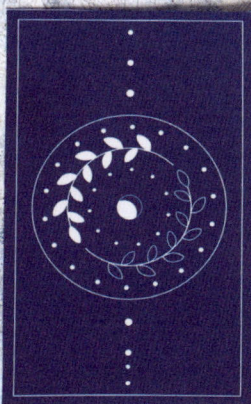

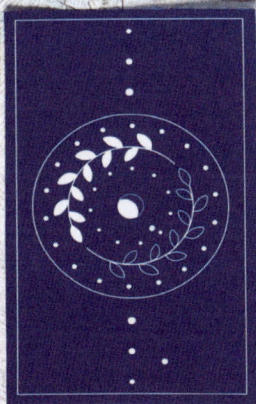

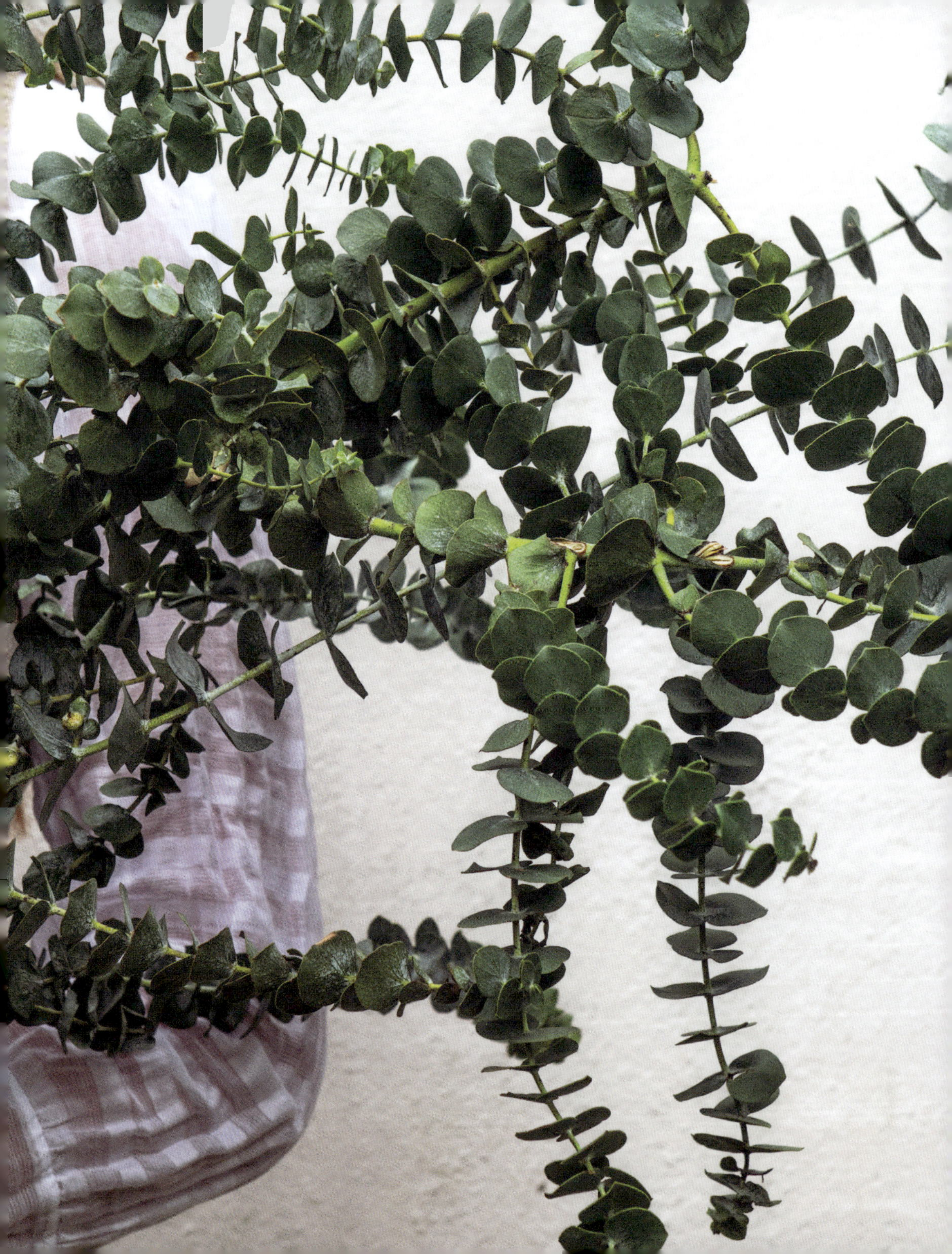

Chapter 1

Embracing the Feminine

Regardless of our gender, we all possess the feminine and masculine within us. But more often than not, we tend to be rewarded for the more masculine expressions of ourselves and we've learned to ignore or override our feminine traits.

For years I tried to suppress my sensitive, introverted, and emotional nature. This manifested in me drinking excessively to calm and quiet my internal world. My emotions bubbled over uncontrollably, and I experienced the ebb and flow of anxiety and depression. I didn't ask for anything, not wanting to appear needy. As a result, I shut people out, struggled to find fulfilling work, and always felt like I was searching for a missing piece that would make me feel happy. Things only began to turn around for me when I acknowledged the feminine piece that had been a part of me the whole time.

When we finally accept our whole self—especially the parts we've rejected—we can show up authentically and start to make magic happen. The strongest way to start this journey to healing through magical self-care is by embracing the feminine—to heal our relationship with it, become whole again, and appreciate and embody the parts of ourselves that are more intuitive, internal, and wild.

Feminine and Masculine

Before we dive deep into the feminine side of life, nature, and healing, let's get clear on some distinctions and definitions. I use the terms feminine and masculine because I resonate with them, but I understand that this duality isn't for everyone.

The terms feminine and masculine are beyond gender, but they often bring up polarizations that some people don't jive with. I include Yin and Yang as maybe not perfect, but closely related and helpful, alternatives.

I think of the feminine as an embodiment of Mother Nature. She nurtures, holds, provides, and accepts, but can show her strength, beauty, and force in powerful and overwhelming ways. She rolls with the seasons and changes with grace, patience, and receptive energy.

Embracing the feminine is about knowing your unique worth and multifaceted power and working with it in a positive way.

The rise of the feminine

Because we live in a society that values the masculine more than the feminine, we've been rewarded and conditioned over time to focus on the masculine qualities of productivity, output, action, and independence. And, as a consequence, we've systematically undermined the feminine traits of feeling, receptivity, and interconnectedness. We've shut down our channel to the gut feelings and heartfelt emotions that live in our bodies.

Collectively, we're ready to turn on our feminine wisdom and intuitive powers and let them help us, which is why all things witchy are coming to the fore. We're shifting out of the masculine-dominated structure to one that incorporates the feminine and seeks a balance and merging of the two.

Why embrace the feminine?

The short answer: to find a better balance in our lives and step into our full power.

While fully embracing the feminine—both within ourselves and out in the world—is a key component of magical self-care, we are ultimately seeking balance between the two. We need both feminine and masculine to be working together in harmony. When we look at the Yin and Yang black-and-white symbol (see opposite), we see the two parts perfectly in balance, a little of the other in each, and meant to fit together.

Forget striving for work/life balance, we should instead seek feminine/masculine balance by finding ways to uncover and work with our feminine side on a daily basis. By nurturing the Yin qualities that we all possess, but which are often underused, we'll begin to find a harmony between the two. When we wake up to the feminine within ourselves, we will be able to realize our full power and creativity as beings on this planet.

With a balance of feminine and masculine you are in flow with your work and life, and acting out of alignment rather than obligation and living out your purpose. It's both giving and receiving in equal measure—filling yourself up so that you can help others.

THE DIFFERENCES BETWEEN MASCULINE AND FEMININE

	Masculine/Yang	Feminine/Yin
Qualities	Refers to the external—action, productivity, rationality, logic, structure, motivation, expression, output, stability, the hustle, and independence	Refers to the internal—intuition, deep feeling, creativity, interconnectedness, cycles, openness, self-worth, wildness, and receptivity
Elements	Fire and air: communication, mental sharpness, ideas, follow-through, dynamic action	Earth and Water: being grounded, emotions, instinct, feelings, soul purpose, nurturing, embodiment
Body	Solar plexus and throat	Heart and gut
Reaction	Speaking	Listening
Cosmic connection	Sun	Moon

JUMP IN: **Embracing the feminine in your everyday life**

Embracing the feminine doesn't have to be all goddess circles, chanting to Kali, or looking at your vulva with a hand mirror (but you totally should if any of those pique your interest). There are plenty of everyday grounded ways to get more in step with our feminine.

★ Getting enough rest
★ Drinking plenty of water
★ Nourishing your body with good food
★ Feeling your feelings
★ Honoring the cycles of your body
★ Having a daily pleasure practice
★ Focusing on the five senses
★ Asking your intuition questions
★ Meditating to quiet the ego and overactive brain
★ Breathing intentionally
★ Movement, such as hip circles, dance, and stretching
★ Sex magic

Honoring your Body

To get in touch with our energy and wisdom, we must honor our body's needs first and foremost. We must give ourselves enough rest, good food, and water to not only function, but thrive. Nurture yourself by asking your body what it needs and really listen to what it is telling you. It's often the simplest things that we need the most. When the body feels properly fed, watered, and rested, it's easier for us to connect to our intuition. That's why I've included recipes in this book—being nourished helps us lay the foundation for hearing our intuition more clearly.

Ask your intuition questions

Your intuition lives in your body, not your rational brain, so your gut or heart are great places to direct your queries. It can be hard to quiet the mind enough to hear an intuitive response, but it can help to start by picturing where your intuition lives.

The main difference between the brain and the intuition is that the intuition is felt. It feels like a knowing and is calmer and quieter than the brain. The brain can often be wrapped up in fear or comparison, so watch out for words and phrases like "should," "need to," or "have to"—these are all clear indicators that the response is coming from your brain. Try meditating or moving your body to clear some space for your intuition to come through, and don't rush or force it.

Intuition answers come quickly and simply, almost like a reflex. Start by training the intuition muscle with simple questions like: "Shall I wear the red or white sweater today?" / "What shall I make for dinner tonight?" / "What route do I want to take to walk home?" Note your first response to these questions and what it feels like when you hear it. Build up to the trickier questions from there.

Feel your feelings

When an emotion arises—good, bad, or neutral—can you just let yourself be with it? Try to avoid finding whys or immediately attempting to fix it. Instead, simply observe it. You can try greeting it if that's helpful, with something like: "Oh hey frustration, I see you've showed up again today—that's cool."

We often try to ignore, rationalize, fix, or tamp down our emotions in order to move past them as quickly as possible, especially the negative ones. But if we can choose to really feel and embrace our emotions fully, and be available for whatever they bring up, we can actually move through them much more effectively than if we just try to ignore them.

Remember: we are not our emotions. This can be hard to remind ourselves of in moments of anger, sadness, or jealousy. This practice of showing up for what we're feeling can help us to separate the self from the emotion.

Instead of letting waves of emotion crash over you, pulling you under or catching you in a rip, learn to ride the wave by being present to what you're feeling and letting it take you along on its journey. Soon the wave will taper off and a new one will come.

This is tough work and *no one* is perfect at it, but if you keep practicing, you'll be able to stay more centered and true to you in all situations, which is the ultimate power stance.

Rest and restore

Resting restores us in so many ways and is just as important as the action phases of our days. It allows us to receive more healing, intuitive hits, and magic in our lives. And while sleep is *so* important—it helps us heal and regenerate more efficiently, enables our brain to function better, and keeps our moods and blood sugar more stable—it shouldn't be the only time we rest.

90/10 work/rest: While working, commit yourself to a 10-minute break every 90 minutes. Do something you enjoy that doesn't require using a computer or phone (playing music is allowed). Take a walk, stare out of the window, do some stretches or breathing exercises, have a snack, or pamper yourself with a face spray or some hand lotion. Repeat throughout your day.

Screen-free time: Screen time does not count as rest. In addition to taking 10 minutes in between working stints, build in screen-free time at the beginning and end of your day. I set my phone to dim all the apps and stay on quiet mode between 8pm and 9am. It's an easy reminder to put the phone down after dinner and until breakfast. This time helps me to be more creative, connect more easily to my partner, and get better sleep.

Meditation: I think that everyone can find a way to meditate that works for them—even if they don't call it that. You can do a walking meditation, a visualization, repeat a mantra, sit and do breathing exercises, or use mindfulness techniques (see below). Choose your own adventure and mix it up. I find that when I'm tired and depleted, even just 5 minutes lying down and breathing mindfully restores me. There are many different meditation techniques, but the goal is to observe your thoughts and eventually calm the mind by separating ourselves from our thoughts.

Mindfulness: One way of being more meditative is through mindfulness. This is the act of bringing your attention to the present moment. You can do this by focusing on your breathing or checking in with all of your senses. What do you hear, see, feel, smell, and taste? You can try a mindful breathing practice, a body scan, or simply go about your everyday chores more mindfully—for example, be more present when you're washing the dishes. Or you might be more attentive in your self-care—for example, being more mindful as you wash your hair and body in the shower and enjoying the sensation of the water, rather than mentally running through your to-do list. Mindfulness can be used as part of a meditation practice as a way to quiet the mind.

Connect with nature: This can serve as brain rest, meditation, and screen-free time. When we see trees, sky, and earth, we feel restored. As someone who lives in a big city, I know this isn't always easy to do, but parks are amazing for this reason. I think connecting to nature even in a small way subconsciously reminds us of our core self and if you can't get outdoors, bring some beautiful house plants into your home.

Try cycle syncing

If you're a bleeding female, I strongly recommend the work of Alisa Vitti, founder of FLO Living, specifically her book *WomanCode*. In it, Vitti details a protocol for working with your menstrual cycle to support your body throughout the month. Cycle syncing is the idea of eating, moving, and working to support your natural cycles, and in turn, letting your cycles and rhythms support you. If you don't bleed or aren't currently bleeding, a similar syncing can be done in accordance to the moon as outlined in the Lunar Living chapter (see page 54).

Because our hormone levels change weekly, depending on where we are in our menstrual cycle, the same food, exercise, and spiritual practices as last week might not work for us this week. We can support ourselves better when we know where we are in our cycle, making us feel more in tune with our body and intuition and enhancing our overall wellbeing.

SUPPORTING YOUR NATURAL CYCLE

	Menstrual (1st day of period–day 7)	Follicular (days 7–14)
Moon phase	New Moon	Waxing
Season	Winter	Spring
Vibe	Inward-focused, connected spiritually, getting pings from the universe, deeply intuitive.	Balanced time between the masculine and feminine. Acting on ideas you had during your menstrual phase, creativity.
Food	Warming, cooked foods, roasted root vegetables, and healthy fats. Dark-hued foods that enrich your iron along with calcium and omega-3s—like beets/beetroot, kale, broccoli, mushrooms, avocado, black lentils, black beans, beef, salmon, chia seeds, berries, pepitas/pumpkin seeds, and linseeds/flaxseeds.	Lightly cooked foods (steam and sauté), sprouted and fermented vegetables. Cooked and raw vegetables along with denser grains and lean proteins. Think foods like raw sauerkraut and kombucha, fresh foods like parsley, salad greens, and cabbage, along with grains farro and oats, plus proteins like eggs, chicken, green lentils, pepitas/pumpkin seeds, and linseeds/flaxseeds.
Movement	Walking, light stretching, rest, and a little yoga later in the phase. Keep it slow.	You have more energy and brain power to take on something new and challenging, so go to that class you've been eyeing and give it a shot.
Self-care practice	Rest. Lay on the couch and read a good book or watch a movie. Buy yourself the fancy tea and (at the risk of being a cliché) the good dark chocolate. Don't feel guilty for taking some time for yourself.	Get out there. Whether you go to a breathwork circle or a new cafe, get out in the world and do something that lights you up. Now is the time to get inspired.

Ovulation (days 14–21)	Luteal (days 21–28+)
Full Moon	Waning/Dark Moon
Summer	Fall
External, action-oriented, full bloom, high energy, making things happen, socializing.	Transformative, releasing what's not serving, fiery, preparing to shed.
Fresh, raw, and lightly cooked foods like vegetable and fruit smoothies, salads, and lighter grains and proteins. Think foods with lots of vitamin C, fiber, and omega-3s. Opt for bitter greens, spinach, red (bell) pepper, tomatoes, strawberries, quinoa, salmon, chia seeds, sunflower seeds, and sesame seeds.	Root vegetables, hearty grains, dark greens. Sauté, roast, and bake. Focus on B and A vitamins, magnesium, iron, and fiber—dark leafy greens, butternut squash, carrots, cauliflower, buckwheat, millet, chickpeas, beef, cod, apples, dates, sunflower seeds, and sesame seeds.
Higher-intensity workouts and cardio—running, cycling, weight-lifting.	Starting to wind down. In the first half, you might still have energy for the higher-intensity activities of the ovulation phase but in the second half, transition to gentler activities such as yoga, walking, and pilates.
Plan a dinner with friends—either at someone's place or out at a restaurant—and spend time connecting, catching up, and storytelling.	A luxurious, tricked-out salt bath—so grab those Epsom salts, skin-safe essential oils, crystals, candles, and whatever else makes you feel like a queen. Go the extra mile for yourself. Soak for a minimum of 30 minutes.
	For recipes ideas for each phase of your cycle, refer to the seasonal recipes on pages 34–41.

Strawberry Beet Power Smoothie

I created this smoothie with the menstrual and follicular phases in mind. It contains beet/beetroot and strawberries which aid depleted iron levels (the strawberries add vitamin C, helping you absorb the iron in the beet more easily), along with lots of fiber from the cauliflower and the seeds for these phases. This smoothie can be enjoyed at other times too, of course.

Makes 1 smoothie

- ☆ 1 beet/beetroot, steamed or roasted and peeled
- ☆ 1 heaped cup/200g frozen strawberries
- ☆ 1 heaped cup/75g frozen cauliflower florets
- ☆ 1 cup/250ml coconut milk
- ☆ 1 tablespoon linseeds/flaxseeds
- ☆ 1 tablespoon pepitas/pumpkin seeds
- ☆ ¼ teaspoon pure vanilla extract
- ☆ granola or hemp seeds, to top (optional)

Blend everything together at high speed in a blender until smooth and creamy. Pour into a glass and enjoy topped with some granola or hemp seeds, or on its own.

Embodiment

The body can hold on to stress, emotions, tension, and pain long after we've experienced a trauma. One way to counteract this is through a regular embodiment practice. Embodiment is a way of feeling into your body. It's a mindful way of coming home to your physical and emotional self, engaging with it, and being open to all of the sensations and feelings it holds. Embodiment practices can look different for everyone, but some include any or a combination of the following:

HIP-CENTERED MOVEMENT

Hip circles, hip swaying, or hip-opener yoga poses are all effective embodiment practices. Our hips, especially as women, are our power source but are often tight especially for those who sit at a desk all day. Doing a few simple hip circles while standing is an easy way to wake them up. Put on a song and circle in one direction and then the other for the duration. Feel into that power source and creativity.

DANCE

I find one of the easiest and most fun ways to get embodied is through expressive movement along with music that makes you feel something—it can be a great release, helping us connect to our body through rhythm, letting us shake and spin things out. Add hip circles for a two-in-one.

BREATHING

We often take in air in quick, shallow breaths while we're simultaneously sucking in our guts. Breathing into our diaphragm and stomach helps enliven our gut and wake up our sacral and solar plexus chakras which house creativity and confidence.

SOUND

Using your voice can be a powerful way of releasing or bringing up stuck emotions. There is no need to say actual words, just make sounds that feel cathartic—whatever comes up and out.

Alexandra Roxo's feminine embodiment practice (see resources, pages 139–140) incorporates breathing, making sounds, and hip circles in a simple routine you can do while lying on your yoga mat. Start with deep belly breaths and long, loud exhales. Then add sounds to your exhales—big sighs, shouts, hisses, laughs, whatever feels right. Then add hip movements in tandem with the other two. This practice is best done with the house to yourself and a playlist turned up loud.

Sex magic

Sexual energy is creative energy. Your sexual energy is often an untapped resource to help enhance your ability to manifest. Owning your sexuality is a way of expressing your power and worth and transforming that energy into something new. Like other forms of energy work, you're harnessing the power of existing energy and channeling it toward something you want. Simply focus on what you're trying to call into your life at the moment of climax, then allow yourself to release it and relax. You can do this with a partner or solo, just make sure you're doing it in a way that feels good to you—whatever makes you feel powerful, comfortable, and aligned is worth doing.

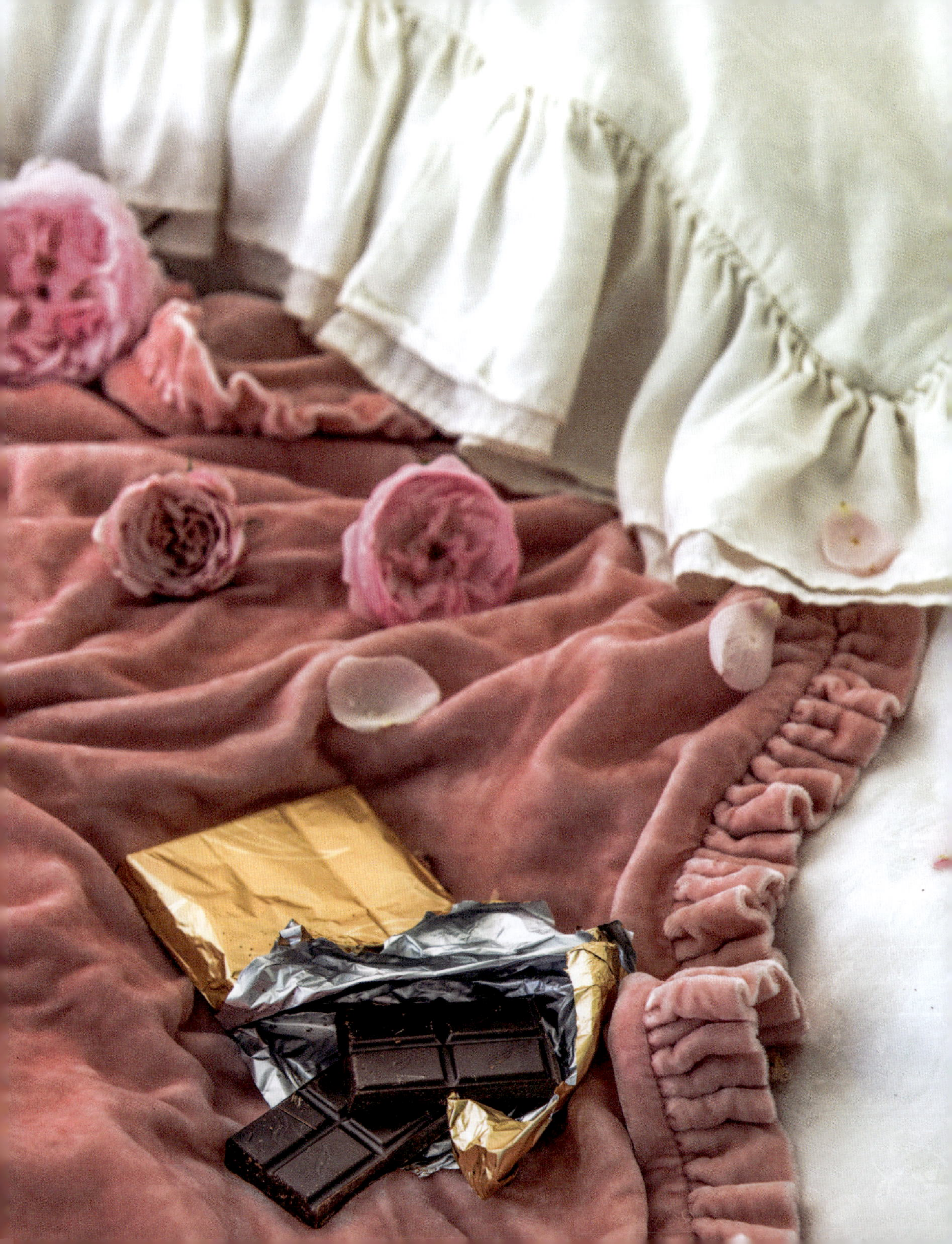

Creating the right ritual for you: Pleasure practice

Cultivating your own pleasure practice will help you tune into your body through the senses. Sensuality, or being in connection to and pleasing the senses, is a big part of the feminine. When we actively engage in our own pleasure—even in tiny, everyday ways —we are showing the universe that we are open to receiving more. Actively pursuing our own enjoyment has the potential to shift our outlook and thought patterns.

Stepping into a headspace of being worthy of receiving good things is one of the best ways we can unlock our magic and magnetic powers. And if you're doing it through a daily pleasure practice, it can be the most fun too. Take a few deep breaths before you start, go slowly, and focus on whatever you're experiencing. The only rule is enjoyment. Switch it up each day to find ways to keep it fresh.

Cooking, dancing, and being in a peaceful natural setting hit most or all of the senses at once. Whatever you decide to do, view your pleasure as an act of pure self-love and liberation. Some areas to explore:

Hear: Music, the ocean, silence, rain.

See: Art, trees, ocean, sunshine, plants, architecture, the farmers' market, loved ones.

Taste: Eat favorite meals and snacks. Buy yourself a fancy version of something you love— chocolate, natural wine, a croissant, a punnet of berries—and take a *looong* time to eat it.

Smell: Essential oils, going to a beloved bakery, making a great cup of coffee, tea, or hot chocolate, fresh flowers or herbs.

Feel/touch: Fresh air, soft or silky fabrics, a warm bath, cuddling a pet, hugging your partner or a friend, massage (self-massage is great for this practice), clean sheets, warm PJs.

Tarot Reflections

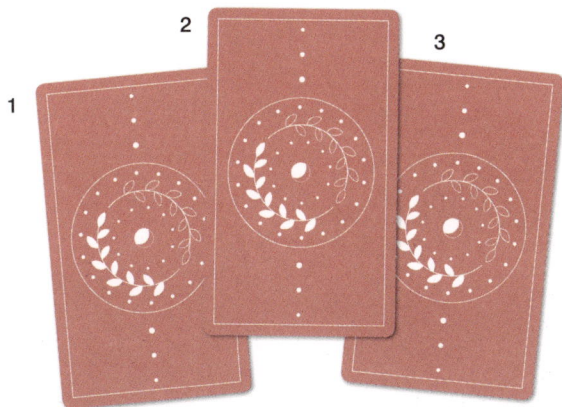

Card 1: What aspect of my feminine side feels neglected?

Card 2: How can I honor my body today?

Card 3: What's one way I can engage in practicing pleasure right now?

See page 11 for guidance.

Chapter 2

Mirroring Nature & the Seasons

Paying attention to the rhythms of the seasons and nature is essential for our health, happiness, and sense of connection.

If we feel at a loss as to what we need or how to care for ourselves, we can simply look to nature as our guide. Mother Nature is our mirror—from the food she provides to the inclination to retreat or expand, she gives us clues to what we need. We just have to look to the weather, plants, or air of a season and respond accordingly.

As a society, we are out of touch with nature's cycles and generosity, and as a result, we're suffering from anxiety, burnout, and disconnectedness— and the planet is suffering too. Rebuilding our relationship with nature and the seasons can help us on an individual, as well as a global, level. The more we focus on having a symbiotic relationship with the rhythms of the Earth, the more we can heal.

Embodying the Four Seasons

Each month and season holds its own magic that becomes obvious when we're in touch with the environment around us. Many of us live in cities or suburbs, so we must seek out pockets of green earth to regularly connect to. Working with the specific shifts of the year is an easy way to start observing the impact that nature can have on us.

Taking some time to really feel into a new season can help us get grounded and bring a new sense of flow into our lives. There's something exciting in the changes from one season to the next. Embody the energy of the current season by mirroring the feeling of it and experiencing all the tastes, scents, and sights associated with it.

EXPERIENCE EVERY SEASON

	SPRING	FALL
Feels like	New life, optimism, emerging, a spark, fresh starts, shifts, crunchy, brightness	A surge of energy, transformation, new directions, possibilities, grounding and warmth
Tastes like	Leafy herbs, baby greens, carrots, radishes, rhubarb, potatoes, light soups, and salads	Squash and pumpkin, dark leafy greens, Brussels sprouts and brassicas, toasted nuts, cinnamon, and nutmeg
Great for	Intention-setting, restarting, activity, creating something new	Shedding what we don't need, fire ceremonies to burn what you're leaving behind, cozy gatherings, sharing food, and nourishment
	SUMMER	WINTER
Feels like	Full bloom, ease, flow, external, abundant, juicy	Quiet, insular, harsh exterior, softness, comforting, and meditative
Tastes like	Tomatoes, stone fruit, berries, melons, summer squash, salads, fresh seafood, cooking on the barbecue, ice cream	Root vegetables, legumes, hardy greens, thick stews, cozy soups, noodles, rice, curries, ginger, cloves, citrus
Great for	Getting out there, adventuring, connecting with others, picnicking	Turning inward, self-care, candle magic, having salt baths

JUMP IN: **Start living with nature as your guide**

There are so many ways you can let nature lead. Here are a few simple ways to connect regularly to nature and the current season:

☆ Commit to daily walks outside (invest in weatherproof shoes and outerwear if you need to—it's worth it)

☆ Find a park (the bigger, the better)

☆ Walk on the grass without shoes when the weather allows

☆ Sit under a tree

☆ Take a day trip to hike or just get out of the city and see some water or trees

☆ Swim in an ocean or lake

☆ Play in the snow

☆ Watch the trees outside your window

☆ Eat outside

☆ Buy food at farmers' markets to get what's really in season

☆ Star- and moon-gaze at night

☆ Make a seasonal to-do list

Explore the elements

Each of the four elements can be found in nature and they are reflected back to us in many forms. The elemental system pops up as a framework in everything from Tarot to astrology to house magic.

Can you explore your relationship to each in a deeper way? Which elements and environments are you drawn to? What does each one make you think of or make you feel?

WATER
Meaning: Our feelings, intuition, emotions, inner world.
Immerse yourself: Get to the ocean, a lake, pond, or river, or just spend time near any of these. Dive in a pool, cry, take an extra-salty bath, or create a sacred shower ritual.

EARTH
Meaning: Our purpose, self-worth, work, abundance, and receptivity.
Immerse yourself: Explore the woods, squish in mud, get lost in a park, look up at big trees and feel the grass beneath your feet, have a picnic, garden, roam.

AIR
Meaning: Our thoughts and the ways we communicate.
Immerse yourself: Simply breathe the air in and notice the shifts in it during different times of year, get up in the mountains or in an open field, coast your bike down a hill, let yourself explore a new place without agenda.

FIRE
Meaning: Our creativity, vitality, motivation and drive, movement, and sexuality.
Immerse yourself: Seek out the desert, tropical heat, simply soak in the sunshine, or hop into a sauna. Do movement that ups your energy and makes you sweat.

Eat with the seasons

Nature is smart—the foods that are in season are exactly what our bodies need for that particular time of year, from juicy hydrating fruit in summer to starchy and filling squash in fall and winter.

Shop at the farmers' market, check labels for locally produced foods at your grocery store, research vegetables and fruits currently in season and build meals around those. Most in-season vegetables and fruits are cheaper than food that has to travel from another climate far away.

Do a digital detox

Whether it's for an afternoon, a weekend, or more, pick a time to delete your social media apps or shut off your phone completely if you can. Technology is amazing, but our devices are keeping us from fully engaging in the world around us. In order for us to connect to our environment and the season, let's step away from our phones and close the laptop, even if it's just for a few moments.

Creating the right ritual for you: The Wheel of the Year

The pagan calendar or Wheel of the Year is a resource for seasonal holidays and feasts. There are many interpretations of these celebrations throughout cultures and history, so seek out ways to celebrate the seasonal shifts that resonate with you. The Wheel includes the equinoxes and solstices as well as holidays in between—each marks energetic shifts throughout the year. For nourishing recipes for each season, see pages 34–41.

Vernal or Spring Equinox/Ostara (Mar 20)

Theme: New beginnings. The transition from winter to spring, the vernal equinox also marks the new astrological year, stepping into the first sign of the zodiac, Aries. There's a balance of light and dark in terms of daylight, marking a potent time of creation, birth, the spark of newness, and honoring the life/death/life cycle.

Honor with: Fresh herbs and flowers, dried herbs and flowers, seeds, candles, fresh air, thinking ahead to what you want to grow in the coming months.

Ask: Where have I transformed and shed in the past 12 months? What's ready to spring forth in my life?

Beltane/May Day (May 1)

Theme: Bursting into bloom. This is a celebration of receiving, fertility, earthly and sensual pleasures, and the divine feminine. The midway point between spring and summer, Beltane is about fun and vibrant celebration.

Honor with: Fire—be it bonfire, barbecue, a candle, or burning herbs; goddess worship; community and/or outdoor celebration; food, drink, music.

Ask: What needs my presence and attention right now? How can I celebrate and honor my body, mind, and spirit connection in an enjoyable way?

Summer Solstice/Litha (June 21)

Theme: Celebrating life and light. This is a joyful time of warmth, sunshine, vibrance, and abundance that serves to honor the longest day of the year. It's about savoring the bright juiciness of the moment with the bittersweet knowledge that each day grows a little darker from this point on. This isn't meant to be depressing, but it should serve as encouragement to luxuriate in what you have when you have it.

Honor with: Time outside, dancing, bonfires, flowers (if ever there was a day for a flower crown, this is it), seasonal food. An evening picnic or barbecue with a view of the sunset is ideal.

Ask: How can I honor my own vibrance in this season? How can I sink into presence more in this very moment?

Lammas (Aug 1)

Theme: Savoring the full bloom. This is a height of summer feast to signify the beginning of the harvest. It's a time of abundance and a time to review and celebrate all the things you've been nurturing since the spring.

Honor with: Bread (signifies the first wheat harvest and makes a good excuse for some summer bruschetta), reflecting on where you've expanded and how far you've come this year, enjoying the weather with others outside.

Ask: What's grown and bloomed in my life in the past few months? What am I most proud of right now?

Autumnal Equinox/Mabon (Sept 22)

Theme: Shedding what's no longer serving you. This mid-harvest marker is about bowing to change, expressing gratitude, and inviting in balance. It's a time for getting closer to who we are at our core.

Honor with: Burning rituals, shadow work (see Chapter 9), home protection magic, gratitude practice.

Ask: Where am I transforming? What needs to be shed to aid my transformation?

Samhain/Halloween (Oct 31-Nov 1)

Theme: Honoring the life/death/life cycle. This is the end-of-harvest holiday that serves as a time of clearings and wrapping things up to make way for what's to come. It's a time when the veil between the spirit world and the earthly realm is the thinnest, making it a good time for honoring our ancestors and spirit guides as we transition into the darker part of the year. It's considered the Witches' New Year, as the earth begins to go dormant.

Honor with: Leaving out gifts for ancestors, guides, and angels. Holding a seance, doing a spirit guide meditation, journaling by asking your intuition questions.

Ask: What's coming to an end in my life right now? What would I like to make more space for?

Winter Solstice/Yule (Dec 21)

Theme: Going inward. A time for reflection, gathering, and connection, the winter solstice kicks off Yule celebrations (which last until the New Year—so you can harness this energy at any point during the Western "Holiday Season.") As the longest night of the year, the solstice invites us to honor the light that's gradually coming back. It's a time of going inward to find what you really, authentically want from your life and how you bring those intentions to life by the spring equinox.

Honor with: Lots of candles/fire; settling intentions for this quiet hibernation time until spring to nurture your

hopes and goals; making manifestation lists; a cozy candlelit dinner with lots of seasonal foods.

Ask: How can I take my self-care to the next level? What will make this cocoon time the most nourishing and nurturing for what I really want to create?

Imbolc (Feb 1)

Theme: Nurturing the seedlings. Think about the seeds you're planting or the ones that are growing roots underground. Think about tending to your personal flame or passion. It's a time of healing and self-care.

Honor with: Taking a cleansing salt bath while practicing gratitude; an energetic and physical space-clearing in your home; doing something artistic that speaks to you.

Ask: How can I tend to my hopes and dreams while doing the same for my body, mind, and spirit?

Tarot Reflections

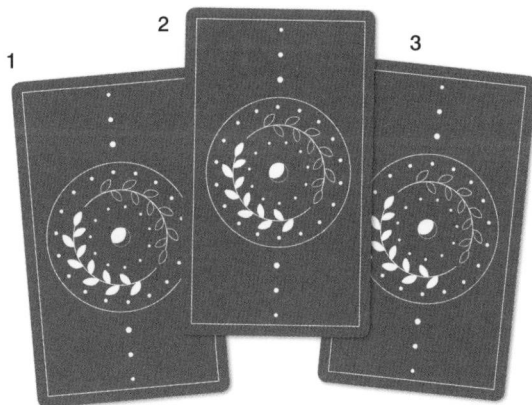

NATURE AND THE SEASONS

Card 1: How can I connect to nature today?

Card 2: What is the theme of this season for me?

Card 3: How can I harness this current season's energy?

See page 11 for guidance.

Spring Equinox Bowl

Hearty grains and roasted carrots meet vibrant herbs and crunchy peppery radishes for a bowl that feels like the transition into spring. At this time of year I'm craving freshness, but still need the grounding coziness of roasted vegetables and some chewy farro/emmer.

Makes 3–4 bowls

* ☆ 1½lb/680g carrots, washed and cut on the diagonal into ovals
* ☆ 2 tablespoons olive oil
* ☆ 1½ cups/270g dry pearled farro/emmer (or substitute with quinoa)
* ☆ 1 large handful of greens (arugula/rocket or baby kale) per bowl, roughly chopped
* ☆ 2 cups/280g cooked chickpeas, drained and rinsed *or* 1 soft-boiled egg per bowl
* ☆ 3–4 radishes, thinly sliced
* ☆ ¼ cup/10g fresh mint, roughly chopped
* ☆ ¼ cup/10g fresh cilantro/coriander, roughly chopped
* ☆ ¼ cup/50g crumbled goat cheese (optional)
* ☆ salt

Tahini herb dressing

* ☆ ¼ cup/50g tahini
* ☆ freshly squeezed juice of ½ lemon
* ☆ 1 tablespoon finely chopped fresh chives
* ☆ ¼ teaspoon garlic powder
* ☆ ¼ teaspoon onion powder
* ☆ ¼ scant teaspoon dried dill
* ☆ salt

Preheat the oven to 400°F/200°C/Gas 6.

Toss the sliced carrots with the olive oil and a generous pinch of salt. Spread the carrots out on a baking tray (you may need to spread between two trays) and roast in the preheated oven for 25–30 minutes, flipping around the 20-minute mark. They're done when they're easily pierced with a fork and golden brown at the edges.

While the carrots are roasting, cook the farro/emmer (or quinoa) according to the package instructions.

Make the dressing by whisking the ingredients together with ¼ cup/60ml water in a small bowl.

If you're including a soft-boiled egg, place the eggs in a pan of cold water, bring to a boil, cover, remove from the heat, and let stand for 6 minutes. Run under cold water, peel, and cut in half.

To serve, combine the greens with a spoonful of dressing and toss to combine. Place in individual serving bowls and top the greens with the cooked farro/emmer, chickpeas or egg, roasted carrots, sliced radishes, and herbs. Drizzle with another couple of spoonfuls of dressing and sprinkle with crumbled goat cheese, if using. Can be served warm or at room temperature.

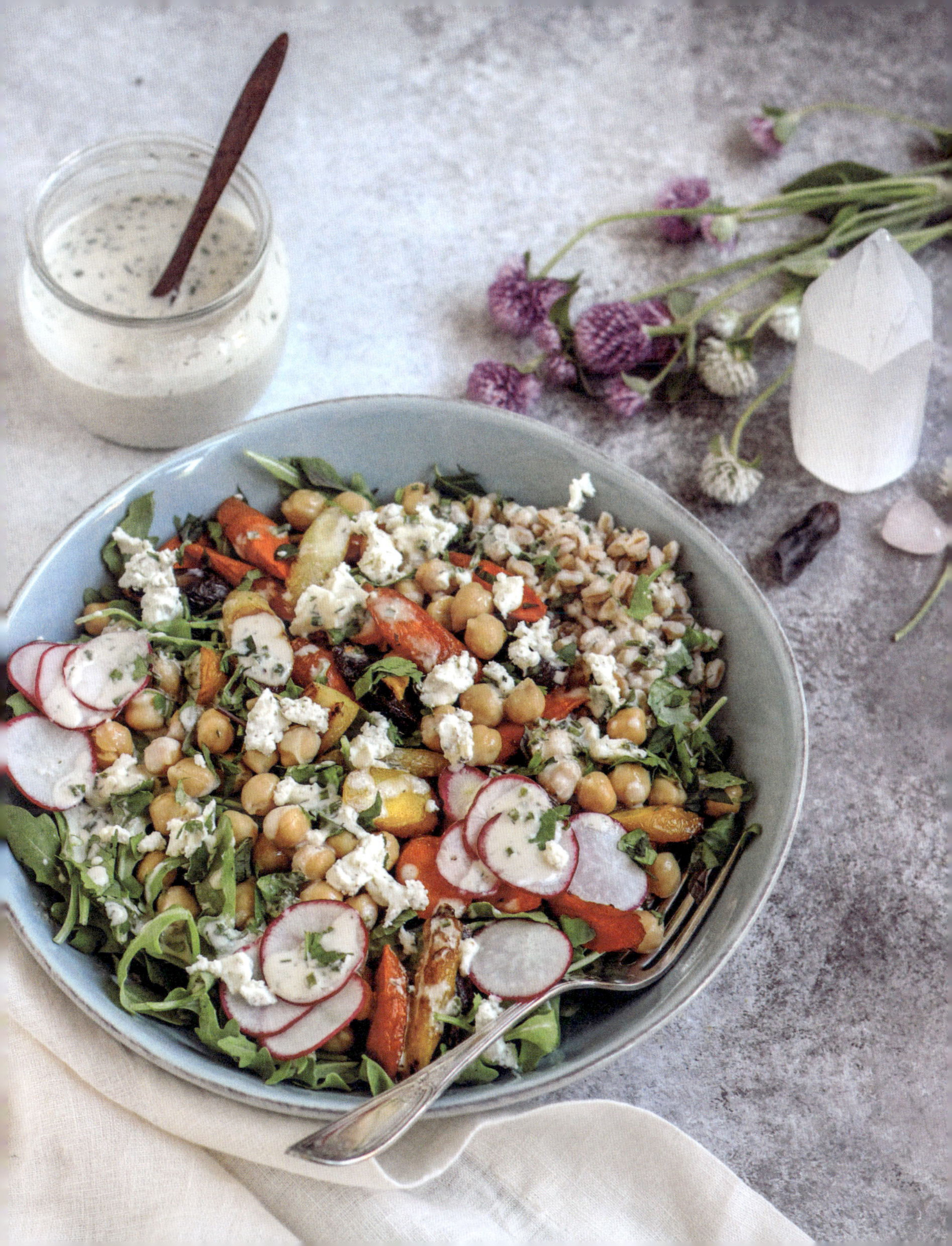

Grilled Veggie Summer Solstice Salad

If you're not a city-dwelling witch and happen to have a barbecue, you can definitely grill the vegetables on there instead of in a skillet/frying pan. If grilling, corn should be kept on the cob and the zucchini/courgettes should be sliced into long, lengthwise strips. Slice the corn kernels off the cob and cut the zucchini after they have been grilled and given some time to cool.

This salad is a great side to any grilled protein, or you can top it with black beans or chickpeas to make it a meal on its own.

Makes 1 big salad, serves about 6 as a side

- ★ 2 tablespoons avocado or olive oil
- ★ 1 medium zucchini/courgette, sliced into small 1-inch/2.5-cm pieces
- ★ 2 ears of corn, kernels cut off the cob
- ★ 1 head of romaine/cos lettuce, washed, dried, and torn or cut into small pieces
- ★ 1 ripe peach or nectarine, pit removed and cut into slices, unpeeled
- ★ 1 avocado, pit removed and cut into chunks
- ★ ¼ cup/5g fresh basil leaves, larger leaves torn
- ★ ⅓ cup/40g toasted pistachios, roughly chopped
- ★ ⅓ cup/45g crumbled feta cheese
- ★ salt

Shallot dijon dressing

- ★ ½ medium shallot, finely chopped
- ★ ¼ cup/60ml olive oil
- ★ 1 tablespoon Dijon mustard
- ★ 1 teaspoon runny honey
- ★ freshly squeezed juice of ½ lemon
- ★ salt and freshly ground black pepper

In a large skillet/frying pan, heat 1 tablespoon of the avocado or olive oil over a medium-high heat. When hot, add the zucchini/courgette and a generous sprinkle of salt and spread into an even layer. Let cook without touching for 3 minutes, then stir and cook for another 2–3 minutes until golden brown and just tender. Remove from the pan and set aside.

Add the remaining tablespoon of oil to the pan. When hot, add the corn and salt to taste. Cook for 3–4 minutes without stirring, then stir and continue to cook for another 3 minutes. Transfer to a plate and set aside.

To make the dressing, place all ingredients in a medium-sized bowl and whisk well to combine.

To assemble the salad, place the lettuce in a large bowl and top with the cooked zucchini/courgettes, corn, peach, avocado, basil, pistachios, and feta. Spoon the dressing over just before serving and toss to combine.

Autumnal Equinox Bowl

This bowl highlights some fall favorites with sweet roasted squash (I suggest a couple of types below, but butternut and acorn squash would both be great as well), fluffy shaved Brussels sprouts, earthy lentils, and crunchy pepitas/pumpkin seeds. I add a spicy smoky chipotle dressing for a vegan bowl that's teeming with flavor to warm you up from the dropping temperatures outside. This dish can be served warm or at room temperature.

Makes 3–4 bowls

* ☆ olive or avocado oil, for greasing
* ☆ 1 medium red kuri squash or delicata squash, seeds scooped out, then cut into wedges or crescent shapes, unpeeled
* ☆ 1½ cups/270g dried black lentils, rinsed
* ☆ ⅓ cup pepitas/pumpkin seeds
* ☆ 1lb/450g Brussels sprouts, trimmed
* ☆ ¼ cup/25g fresh parsley, roughly chopped
* ☆ salt

Chipotle-cashew dressing

* ☆ 1 chipotle pepper in adobo sauce
* ☆ 1 tablespoon adobo sauce
* ☆ freshly squeezed juice of ½ lime
* ☆ 2 tablespoons raw cashews
* ☆ 1 date, pitted (can substitute honey or maple to taste)
* ☆ salt

Preheat the oven to 375°F/190°C/Gas 5.

Grease a baking tray with oil and arrange the squash slices on it in a single layer. Sprinkle with salt and bake in the preheated oven for 40–45 minutes until tender, rotating the tray at the 20-minute mark.

Place the lentils in a saucepan with 4 cups/1 litre water and a generous pinch of salt, cover, and bring to boil. Reduce to a simmer and cook for 20–25 minutes, or until the lentils are tender but still maintaining their shape. Drain and set aside until you're ready to use.

Toast the pepitas/pumpkin seeds in a dry skillet/frying pan over a low heat for 5–8 minutes, or until they start to turn golden and/or pop. Remove from the heat and let cool before using them.

Shave the Brussels sprouts on a mandoline or slice very thinly with a knife.

Make the dressing by blitzing everything together in a blender with ½ cup/120ml water, adding more water if necessary to get desired consistency.

To assemble, divide the shaved Brussels sprouts between the bowls and drizzle with a little dressing. Top with lentils, squash, pepitas/pumpkin seeds, and parsley and spoon over more chipotle dressing.

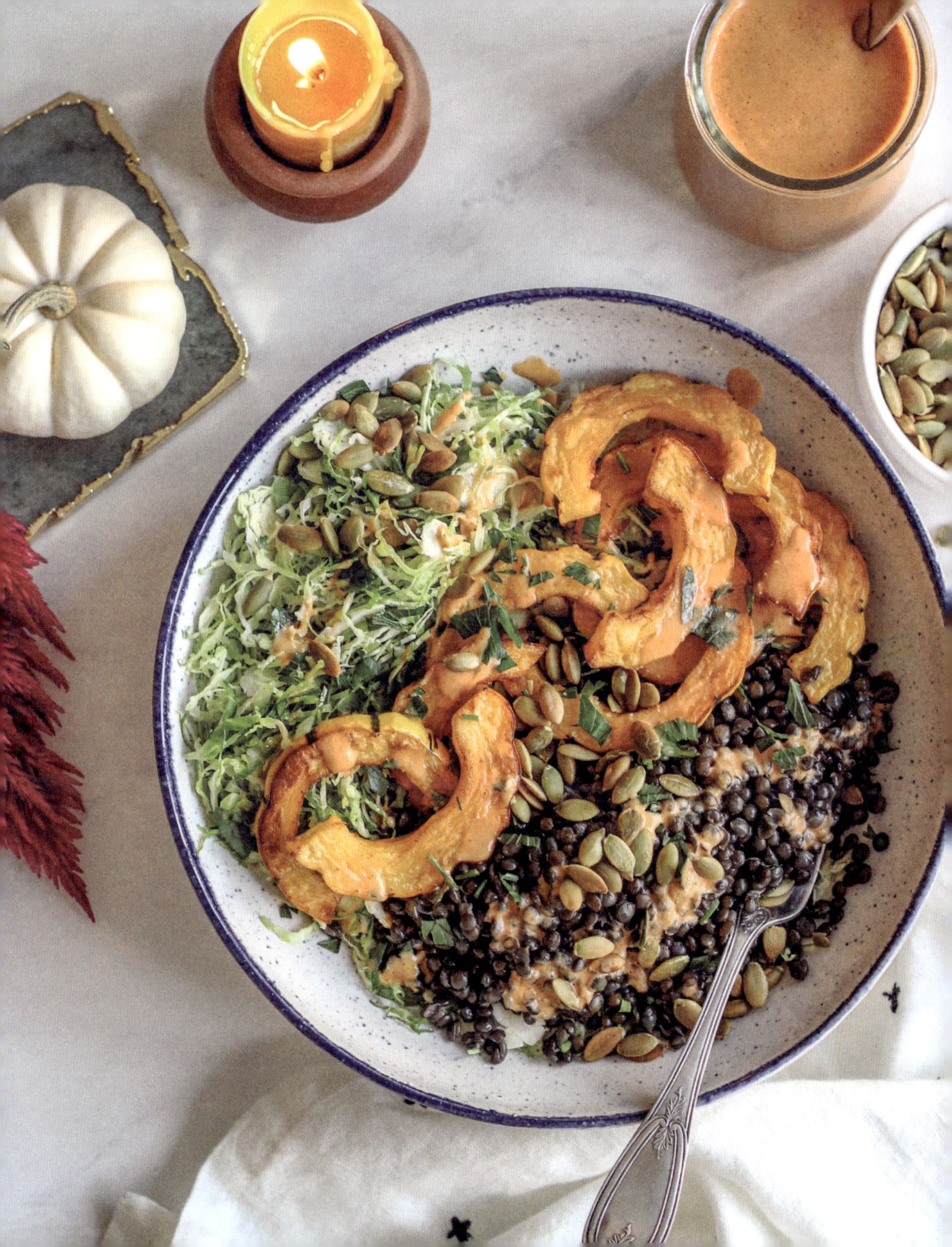

Winter Solstice Soup

As this puréed soup is pretty monochrome, I love adding pops of color and texture in the toppings, whether with hot pepper/chilli flakes, fresh herbs, or roasted kale chips. Celery root/celeriac and potatoes represent the roots we'll be tending to in winter as we go inward. If you can't find celery root, feel free to replace with two medium bulbs of fennel. Any white bean can be used, such as cannellini beans or navy/haricot beans (remember to soak them beforehand). Be sure to serve with any toppings you'd like and good crusty bread.

Serves 6

* ☆ 1 head of garlic
* ☆ 3 tablespoons grass-fed butter or olive oil, plus extra oil for greasing
* ☆ 2 leeks, trimmed, cleaned, and thinly sliced
* ☆ 2 medium celery root/celeriac, peeled and cut into chunks
* ☆ 2 medium white potatoes, peeled and cut into chunks
* ☆ 1 cup/175g dried white beans, soaked in water overnight or for at least 4 hours
* ☆ 6 cups/1.5 litres chicken or vegetable broth
* ☆ 1 teaspoon sherry vinegar
* ☆ salt and freshly ground black pepper

Topping ideas

* ☆ roasted kale chips
* ☆ toasted pine nuts or slivered almonds
* ☆ crumbled chorizo, browned, to taste
* ☆ red pepper/chilli flakes
* ☆ fresh parsley or chives, roughly chopped

Preheat the oven to 375°F/190°C/Gas 5.

Cut the woody base off the head of garlic using a sharp knife. Drizzle a small amount of olive oil on a small square of kitchen foil, place the cut side of the garlic down on the oil and wrap the foil tightly around the garlic. Roast in the preheated oven for 40–45 minutes until fragrant and the cloves are completely soft. Set aside to cool.

Heat the butter or olive oil in a large soup pot or dutch oven. Add the leeks and cook, stirring regularly, over a gentle heat for about 5 minutes until softened. Add the celeriac and potatoes and cook for another 5 minutes, stirring occasionally. Drain the white beans from their soaking water, then add the beans and broth into the soup pot, along with the roasted garlic cloves (squeeze each softened clove out from the papery skins). Bring everything to the boil, then cover and cook, at a simmer, stirring occasionally, for 45–55 minutes until the beans are tender.

Purée the soup using an immersion blender or in batches in a standing blender until smooth. Stir in the sherry vinegar and season to taste. Serve hot with desired toppings.

Chapter 3

Creating a
Magical Home

Maybe it's because I'm a Cancer Rising, Taurus Moon, or an introvert, but my home is really important to me. It took me years to realize this, but once I prioritized creating a home I love, my spiritual practice started to flourish. A magical home is a space that helps you come back to yourself and makes you feel good. What we're aiming for is a calming, grounding, and safe place where you can spend time alone and with the people you love. It's where you'll do the majority of your everyday magic, so it's important that this space feels unique to you and uplifting. It's about creating an energy that supports you and helps you click into your most authentic self when you step through the door. Infusing your home with positive intentions, regularly clearing physical and energetic clutter, and creating a supportive, healthy, and beautiful environment will nurture you and help you get the most out of your self-care. In fact, just being in your magical home can feel like self-care.

Your Magical Home

When we set up our space to be a reflection of what makes us feel safe, joyful, and peaceful, it helps us access our authentic core self. Being connected to that core is vital for magic and manifesting what you want for yourself. A witchy home can help you come home to yourself, allowing you to feel fully comfortable in your body and spirit.

Creating a magical home (and by home, I mean anything from your bedroom if you have roommates, to an entire house—whatever space you call your own) is very subjective and will look different for everyone. But to get you started, here are some basics on how to set up a space that feels functional, positive, and supportive to you and your life.

Cleanse and clear

The biggest issue with a lot of our spaces is the stuck, stale feeling that accumulates along with all of our stuff. The quickest way to banish this feeling is to get rid of the clutter. You don't need a rigorous protocol—go at your own pace, room by room, or category by category—and donate, recycle, or give away anything that you don't use regularly or simply hate looking at. Designate a place for everything you decide to keep. Often just finding baskets and boxes to contain objects that are usually kept out can create a sense of calm and order. All objects should have a home within your home.

Do a clean-out each season just before the solstice (see page 32) or equinox (see page 33), shedding what you don't need and making space for what's to come. Not only will this clearing make your home look and feel more serene, but it will energetically open your home up for more of what you're calling in. You're showing the universe that you're ready for change and willing to take action toward your own well-being.

SMOKE CLEANSING

To clear energetic clutter, try smoke cleansing. You can burn sticks of wood such as Palo Santo, or herbs such as rosemary or sage. Some herbs like white sage and palo santo are overharvested, so many ready-made bundles aren't the best for the environment or the plant.

If you want to buy these, make sure that they are ethically harvested or wildcrafted. Mountain Rose Herbs is a great resource for this (see page 139).

Cleanse your space as often as you feel is necessary. Energy from bad moods and stress can linger in our spaces—a combination of smoke and fresh air can help us reset.

Sage: For purification, longevity, protection, wisdom, clean slate, neutralizing, and clearing all energy.

Palo Santo: For positivity, spiritual protection, purification, healing, creativity, smoothing and balancing energy.

Rosemary: For clarity, mental fortification, purification, healing, protection.

Juniper: For protection, love, health.

Sweetgrass: For calling in good spirits, healing, peace, spirituality.

Mugwort: For strength, psychic connection, healing, protection.

Thyme: For health, healing, love, courage.

Lavender: For peace, sleep, protection, purification, love, happiness.

How to choose: You can either pick which properties resonate with you or just go on scent alone. The smell will be filling your home, so it's an important factor. Take whichever scent you're drawn to as a sign that you're meant to work with it.

JUMP IN: **Working with your home's energy**

You can do these things in order, start with what excites you, or what you know you need to focus on.

Add more magic energy to your space by:

☆ Clearing and cleansing both clutter and energy

☆ Healing yourself with kitchen witchery and creating a home apothecary

☆ Enhancing your unique magical environment with candles, crystals, color, and more

Make your own cleansing bundles

You'll need

☆ Stalks of fresh herbs (see page 44)

☆ Cotton string: choose a particular color to imbue your bundle further (see page 51) or go with what you have in your home.

How to do it: Gather together sprigs of herbs that are a similar size. Line up all stems with one another evenly, leaves facing up.

Tie the stems tightly with your string, encircling the stems a few times and making a few knots. The herbs will shrink as they dry, so the tighter the better. Then crisscross the string around the herbs, down the length of the springs, bundling them together tightly as you go. Finish toward the other end of your bundle and trim your string.

You can begin to use these at any time, but dried works best. Hang your herb bundle upside down in a dry place for several weeks, until you're ready to use. Follow the smoke-cleansing instructions below to use.

How to smoke cleanse

1. Pick the herb or wood you'd like to use. Make a bundle (see above) if you're starting with your own herbs.
2. Light it at the end, gently blow on it to let the flame die down to a low and slow kind of burn that smokes.
3. Burn it in each room, outlining the space, from corner to corner and around the windows and doors. Go low to the ground, since smoke rises anyway. The smoke will cleanse the air and the aura of the space as you go.
4. As you're going around your home think or say out loud the intention you have for your home. Try: "I release negativity and anger from this home" / "Protect this home from future clutter and chaos" / "I balance and recharge this home with love."
5. End at the front door of your home. Extinguish the smoke by firmly stamping your bundle or wood out on a fire-resistant surface (I have a shell for this) while letting your intention go. Take a big breath and open the windows to bring in fresh air and energy.

SALT AND SALT WATER

Salt and salt water are powerful cleansing tools. For cleansing a specific object, like a crystal or a Tarot deck, you can simply place it in a bowl full of sea salt.

To cleanse your body, take a salt bath. Epsom salts are rich in magnesium and help to draw those stagnant and generally "blah" feelings out of you. Draw a circle of salt around you and/or your altar when you're setting intentions or doing a spell.

Heal

Using everyday activities around the home to heal or help is one of my favorite forms of magic. By cooking and choosing ingredients with specific intentions in mind, we can improve our mental and physical health and make these daily actions more fun.

Kitchen witchcraft

Kitchen witchery is one of the easiest forms of magic to practice if you already cook—even just a little. We already have most of the kitchen tools we need to perform this magic—we simply need to add some food and intention.

Being a kitchen witch is the practice of imbuing the food you cook with positive intentions and healing properties. It's a way of caring for yourself and others with thoughtfulness and nourishment. What we eat and how we eat it becomes part of us, fueling our cells and energy. If we're fed well with food and intentions that uplift, comfort, and support us, we will have a beautiful base for healing and tapping into the soul wisdom that lives in our bodies.

Infuse your food with intentions: Decide how you want to feel during and after eating. Once you know what you're aiming for, choose food that reflects your purpose (like roast potatoes for comfort, chocolate for pleasure, chicken vegetable soup for soothing etc.) and continually bring your focus back to your intention while preparing.

Use cooking to release tension and emotion: Use the acts of tearing, chopping, or peeling to strip away the day so far. Imagine the frustrating parts being torn or shed. Say goodbye to the day as you place food into a hot pan to be transformed into something delicious.

Moving meditation: If you continually come back to your intention or purpose for the food, it can create a mindful or meditative practice out of preparing meals.

Make your blade or wooden spoon your magic wand: As you use these kitchen tools, think of them as conductors of the energies you're trying to infuse into your food. As you slice, stir, and sauté with them, imagine your purpose filling the food that they touch.

Serving it up: Make your food look as special as it was intended to be. Serve it in a favorite ceramic bowl or take special care to garnish with fresh herbs, toasted nuts and seeds, and cracked pepper. Serving food with joy and care really drives home your initial aim.

Home apothecary

Having herbs, spices, and plants on hand to help heal common issues—from cuts and scrapes to colds and headaches—is a great way to get practical with your magic. For more on home apothecary, see Chapter 7.

ESSENTIAL OILS
Tea tree: Antibacterial and drying. Use a little on cuts, pimples, and ingrown hairs.
Cinnamon: A powerful anti-inflammatory and fights infection, so it's great for cuts and scrapes.
Peppermint and lavender: Help ease headache pain when rubbed on the temples and back of neck.
Eucalyptus: Helps with congestion. Place a couple of drops in the palm of your hands, cup around your nose and mouth, and breathe in deeply, or pour a few drops in the shower and let the steam do the rest.

SPICES
Anti-inflammatories: Cinnamon, cumin, turmeric
Digestive aids: Fennel, coriander, cardamom
Immunity: Cayenne, cloves, ginger, thyme

Enhance and Create

Now it's time to up the vibe. Discover how to improve the feeling of your home and imbue it with magic with these simple tools.

Scent

Scent can change the feeling of a room. Try essential oils like sweet orange, neroli, and grapefruit for being uplifted, lavender and sandalwood for chilling out, and peppermint and rosemary for improving focus. Experiment to find what scents you love by going to a shop and sniffing a wide selection of pure, organic essential oils. I buy most of mine on Mountain Rose Herbs (see page 139) or Thrive Market.

Enhance the mood of your home through scent by making your own room sprays, diffusing oils, arranging flowers, plants, and herbs, and cooking with or using sweet-smelling spices on the stovetop.

Easy room refresher: In a small saucepan, combine ¼ teaspoon each of cinnamon and allspice and a piece of orange peel. Cover with water and simmer for an hour or two and the spicy-sweet scent will spread throughout your home. Top up the water if it gets low in the pan.

Room spray: In a glass spray bottle, combine 3-4 oz of witch hazel, filtered water, or vodka and 10–20 drops of essential oils of your choosing and shake with the lid on to combine. Spray around as needed.

Candle magic

Candles are all four elements in one—the fire and air reinforce your intention and the melted and solid wax represent the intuitive water and grounded earth. Place a white candle on your altar or in a special place in your home. As you light it, think about what you're calling in. Or write it out and place the paper beneath the candle. Let the candle burn out completely. You can also use a colored candle that corresponds to what you're calling in (see page 51) or carve a word or symbol that represents your intention into the candle before burning.

Crystals

While crystals won't solve your problems, they do bring certain vibrations with them and can reinforce your intentions—both holding space for them and serving as a visual reminder of what you're calling in or changing.

To pick the right crystals, simply recognize those you're attracted to. You'll be drawn to the right ones for your home and life. They'll likely be ones you find beautiful, which will add to your space in a positive way.

LIVING ROOM/COMMUNAL AREAS

Black Tourmaline: Clears negativity and bad thought patterns, reduces impact of electromagnetic radiation from phones and computers, and reduces stress.
Citrine: Optimism, creativity, confidence, sunshine.
Selenite: Cleanses, clears, protects, light bringing, guidance.
Smoky Quartz: Letting it go, harmonizing, detoxifying, focus.

BEDROOM

Amethyst: Spiritual connection, intuition, protection, anxiety-reducer.
Carnelian: To ignite passion, but don't keep near your bed when you want to sleep as it can boost your energy.
Celestite: Healing sleep, gentle dreams, deeply calming, antidepressant, universal wisdom.
Moonstone: Divine feminine energy, soothing, balancing.
Rose Quartz: Warm and loving energy, coziness, calming.

KITCHEN

Carnelian: Boosting metabolism, vitality, energy, passion, courage, confidence.
Green Jasper: Grounding energy, nutrient absorption.
Green Aventurine: Easing stress and anxiety, luck, heart

opening, connecting you to healing Earth energy.
Rose Quartz: Self-love, gentle, heart-centered energy.

OFFICE

Citrine: Abundance, success, positivity, the bright side, manifestation.
Clear Quartz: Clarity, focus, healing, enlightened thinking.
Labradorite: Curiosity, universal connection, magic, clairvoyance, psychic abilities.
Lapis Lazuli: Awareness, wisdom, soul purpose guidance.
Shungite: Protects from EMFs from technology, absorbs negativity, purifies.
Sodalite: Aligning with your purpose, communication, intuition, organization.

CRYSTAL-INFUSED WATER

Create this to use crystals and play with their energy. Google your crystal to make sure it's not water-soluble, then clean it with dish soap or by soaking in salt water. Hold the crystal in your hand and think about what it means to you. Combine 4 cups/1 litre filtered water and crystal in a jar or bottle and let it sit overnight to infuse the water with the crystal's energy. Sip with a straw, topping up with more purified water throughout the day, without letting the crystal water ever fully run out.

Music

Music changes the energy of a space. Create playlists for different moods and times (for cooking, meditation, date night) to conjure up a specific ambiance quickly.

Beauty

In order for your home to feel like a reflection of your core self, it should have things that you find beautiful. Start small and highlight what you already have. A few things that make a big difference to a space:

LIGHTING

Natural lighting during the day and low lighting once the sun has set help our body clocks find their natural rhythm. Himalayan pink salt lamps are said to help naturally cleanse the air and create a gorgeous blush-colored glow. You can also use incandescent bulbs, small table lamps, twinkle lights, and candlelight in combination for your ideal glow.

COLOR

Color can have a huge impact on your mood, which makes sense because each color holds its own magic. Choose a couple of colors to form the base palette of your home and incorporate a power/accent color to weave throughout. You can do this room by room or for the home overall. Color meanings can be very individual to a person, so take these following associations only as a jumping off point.

Red: Vibrance, security, passion
Orange: Creativity, motivation, energy
Yellow: Warmth, happiness, intelligence
Green: Grounded, earthy, serene, abundance
Blue: Calm, communication, wisdom, peace
Indigo: Spirituality, rebelliousness, playful
Purple: Dreams, psychic connection, power
Pink: Love, tenderness, joy, kindness
White: Clean slate, peace, intuition
Gold: Luxury, warmth, abundance
Black: Grounded energy, protection, stress banishing
Gray: Soothing, softness, balancing
Silver: Lunar energy, intuition, emotional balance
Coral: Playfulness, cheer, positive energy
Turquoise: Loving, open-heartedness, optimism

PLANTS

Greenery can do wonders for air quality and your general mood. Succulents near the entrances and just outside of the home can protect a home and promote positive vibes. Air purifiers like snake plants, ferns, and peace lilies are all excellent choices keeping airflow clean and balancing energy.

Creating the right ritual for you: Altar-building

An altar is a space to remind us of our intentions, and where we do magic, meditate, pray, or recenter. Your altar can be on a tray in your kitchen, a bedside table, a windowsill—anywhere. It doesn't have to be big—it's simply a space that's yours to decorate as you see fit.

Customize this ritual to include any tools or objects that you love—get creative.

1. Around the time of the New Moon (the beginning of a new cycle), think of what you'd like to focus on in the month ahead.
2. With your new intention in mind, find items you'd like to include on your altar to remind you of this intention. Use Tarot or goddess cards, crystals, sea shells, wildflowers, leaves, plants, candles, jewelry, or handwritten mantras. Pick about three special items to start—you can always add to it later.

3. Clean your altar space, remove all items that were on it previously, and give it a good scrub. Now's a great time to smoke or salt cleanse the space, too.
4. Arrange your altar with the new items you've gathered. As you place each item on the altar, think about what it represents in relation to your intention. See your intention fully becoming a part of your life. Feel what it feels like.
5. Seal your new altar with a gratitude practice for the cycle that's passed and by lighting a candle.

You can do this ritual over a few days.

Tarot Reflections

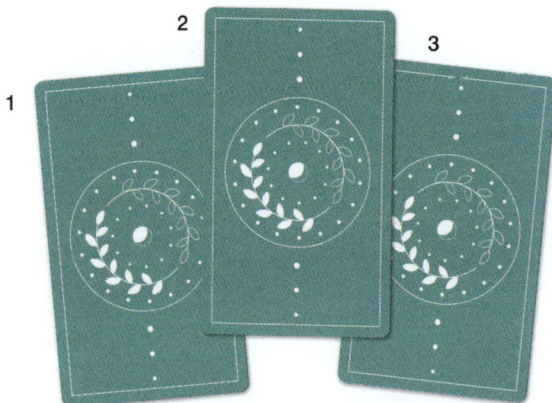

Card 1: What energies are currently at play in my home?
Card 2: What would feel good to let go of?
Card 3: What intention or energy would feel good to welcome in at this time?

See page 11 for guidance.

Almond Butter Tahini Success Cookies

Baking has its own form of magic that creates sweetness and warmth in the home. Sesame seeds (which is what tahini is made from) and almonds represent success and abundance.

Makes 12 cookies

☆ 2 eggs (US large/UK medium) or 2 chia eggs (2 tablespoons ground chia seeds + 6 tablespoons water)
☆ 1 cup/225g natural almond butter, stirred well
☆ ½ cup/100g tahini, stirred well
☆ ½ cup/100g coconut sugar (or use brown sugar)
☆ 1 teaspoon baking powder
☆ ½ teaspoon pure vanilla extract
☆ sea salt flakes
☆ ½ cup/70g roughly chopped dark chocolate

In a large bowl, beat the eggs (or combine chia seeds and water and allow to stand for 5 minutes). Add the almond butter, tahini, coconut sugar, baking powder, and vanilla extract, and stir well to combine (I like to use a rubber spatula for this). Place in the fridge while you preheat oven.

Preheat the oven to 375°F/190°C/Gas 5. Line a baking tray with parchment paper.

Roll spoonfuls of dough into balls slightly smaller than a ping pong ball and evenly space them on the tray (I can usually fit 12 cookies on a large-sized baking tray). Gently press each ball down with a fork one way and then the other to create a grid pattern. Sprinkle a pinch of sea salt flakes on each cookie.

Bake in the preheated oven for 10–12 minutes. Allow to cool on the tray for at least 10 minutes before transferring to a plate or wire rack to cool completely (they're more likely to fall apart if you don't give them this cooling time on the tray).

Cover a plate with parchment paper (you can reuse the parchment from baking). Gently melt the chocolate in a double boiler or in a heatproof bowl placed over a pan of simmering water, and remove from the heat once completely melted.

Dip the cookies half-way in the chocolate and transfer to the parchment-lined plate. Let cool until hardened and enjoy.

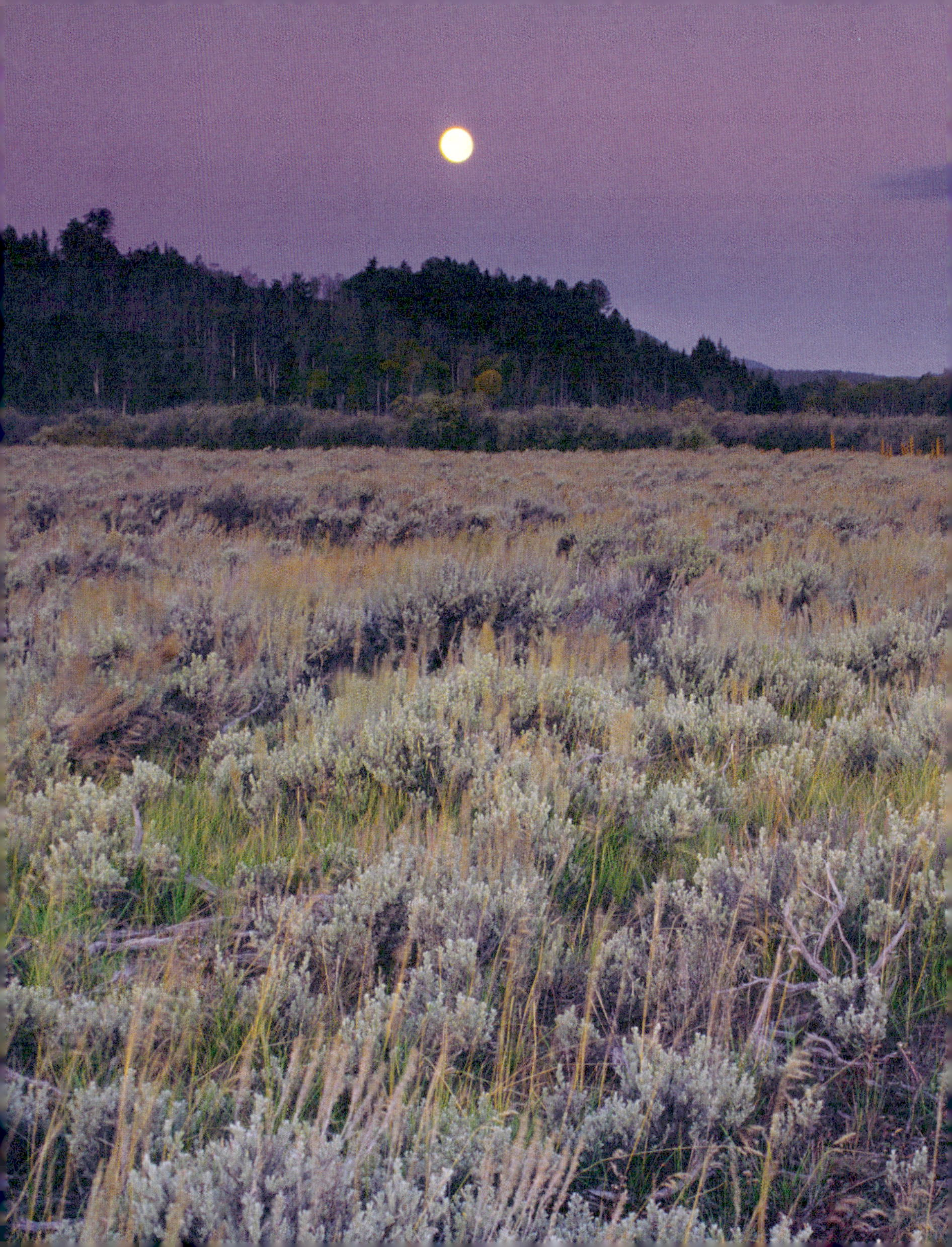

Chapter 4

Lunar Living

Lunar Living is a way of moving through the world in alignment with the moon cycles. It's being aware of what phase the moon is in and planning accordingly, based on the effect it has on you personally. Some people might ask, "Why work with the moon?" My first reaction to this is: Why not? These roughly month-long cycles are an ideal timeframe for checking in with yourself, if nothing else. Using this orb in the sky to help you connect to the bigger picture and the deeper, more subconscious parts of yourself can be kept as simple or as meaningful as you'd like. It can be a daily visual reminder to check in with yourself or you can use it as a guide for your transformation and evolution. You get to decide what it means to you.

For example, the Waning Moon, which comes right before a new cycle and therefore a New Moon, is often a time when we feel more introverted, internal, and quiet and may prefer some time to ourselves to rest. If we know this in advance, we can plan to stay in on the night or two leading up to the New Moon. We can use that time to journal, cook ourselves a meal, or take an Epsom-salt-heavy bath.

Lunar living doesn't have to look like howling at or dancing naked under the Full Moon (but if you're called to that, DO IT!)—it just means that you're aware of the impact the moon can have and you look to it to help you check in with yourself and meet your needs.

Working with the Moon

The subconscious is what drives us. It's what we feel on a deep level, but we rarely pay it the attention it deserves, which means we are on autopilot most of the time. The moon represents our subconscious, intuition, moods, and inner knowing. Choosing to work with the moon puts us more in touch with these intangible, fluid parts of ourselves and in a position to work with them. When we dig into the subconscious, we have the power to shift the way we think and operate in everyday life.

If you choose to use the moon as a guide for self-care and taking action, you will begin to see changes in your life. By thinking about what you want and using the cycle to call it in, take steps forward, rest, call out what's not serving you, and (most importantly) work with the deepest parts of yourself, you'll start to see your own personal evolution taking hold.

The Yin and Yang of the cycle

There is a push and pull to the moon's energy, much like the tides it controls. We can use the moon phases to create a balance of the Yin (feminine, receiving) energy and the Yang (masculine, doing) energy (see page 15). Ezzie Spencer's book *Lunar Abundance* covers this concept in depth, and I highly recommend you read it if working with the moon interests you.

Most of us tend to be Yang or masculine dominant. This has nothing to do with gender, but with the action-oriented, doing/productivity/hustle-focused nature of working and living in our modern world. Even leisure activities and relaxing need to be captured and captioned for Instagram—it feels like we can no longer just be and enjoy.

Working with the moon as our guide helps us establish a rhythm of resting, surrendering, and receiving in tandem with doing, seeking, and making. Each of the eight phases alternate between Yin and Yang, creating this push-pull, action-rest rhythm.

Accessing your intuition

We need quiet time, even just a few moments, to come back to ourselves and let the quiet voice of intuition speak to us. The chatter of the mind can be so loud and constant that any way we can find a slice of silence is restorative. The moon can provide this quiet time, whether you're gazing up at it on a clear night or feeling into that particular phase.

The cycles

The moon moves through eight main phases in a cycle, which is roughly 29 days long, with each phase lasting three-and-a-half days. Often, you'll see these phases reduced to four on calendars, but the eight really capture the intricacies of the cycle. That being said, eight is a lot, so if you can only handle checking in on the New and Full Moons, that's great too.

NEW MOON

The start of a new cycle. This is the time when the moon is barely visible in the sky. It's a time of beginnings, fresh starts, and new energy.

WAXING CRESCENT

The moon has grown into a pretty crescent at this time and the energy for supporting your intention is building.

FIRST QUARTER MOON

We're halfway to the Full Moon now and gaining momentum with our intention.

WAXING GIBBOUS

The moon is almost full in the sky—energy is heightened and there is a palpable excitement.

FULL MOON

The moon is at its most brilliant and attention-grabbing at this time. You might feel the same—wanting to get out there and socialize, connect, or share what's in your heart and mind. You could also feel more emotional or intense than usual. This is an expansive time—whatever it makes you feel, fully show up for it.

WANING GIBBOUS

The moon is slowly beginning to decrease from its full size. You might feel emotional after the high of the Full Moon or the pull to recharge.

LAST QUARTER

We're at that half-moon point again—paring back toward the new moon with less of the moon visible in the sky. You may start to see which patterns or habits are serving you and which aren't.

WANING MOON OR BALSAMIC MOON

The moon is back to a crescent form again, preparing for a new cycle, but still finishing out the current one. This period of time covers the Dark Moon in the day or so before the New Moon, which can be a particularly low-energy, introspective time.

Check the astrology of each moon

One of the most interesting things I've found in working with the moon is incorporating the astrology of each moon. The moon moves through every sign of the zodiac in one cycle, spending approximately two-and-a-half days in each sign.

Not only can the astrology sign of a New Moon or Full Moon serve as a guide if you're having trouble landing on an intention, but it can provide an interesting lens to look at the energies at play. A Leo Full Moon has a very different vibe to a Pisces Full Moon, which keeps things exciting and gives the year a certain cadence to it. For your individual moon sign, check out Chapter 5.

Why is getting your period sometimes called your moon cycle?

Some people call their period their moon cycle. If you think of the New Moon as the beginning of your cycle, followed by the energy build up of the follicular phase, peaking at the Full Moon or ovulation (when you're at your most fertile), then the gradual shedding of the Waning Moon, into the low-energy time of the Dark Moon, just before or at the start of your period, when the cycle begins again (see chart on pages 20–21). Whether you're a menstruating woman or not, the moon can help you go deeper into the natural rhythms within yourself.

JUMP IN: **How to start working with the moon**

A great way to start using the moon to check in with yourself and your needs is to create a simple ritual.

1. **Look:** Start checking the moon at night. Notice what it looks like and look up the phase that it's currently in. You can add this to your online calendar or use apps for a quick reference.

2. **Feel:** Pay attention to the ebb and flow of how you feel during the moon cycle. Jot down a few words on a planner or calendar, or in a journal, about how you feel.

3. **Set an intention:** At the New Moon or in the days after, sit down in a quiet spot and think about what you'd like more of in your life. Create a simple, easy-to-remember intention for the cycle ahead. Don't worry if you don't hit the New Moon exactly—you can set an intention at any point in the cycle as needed.

4. **Check in:** Keep checking in on your intention and yourself throughout the cycle—once a week is great. How can you take action on your intention and how can you make room for it in your life?

5. **Make it special:** Now that you're getting into the flow of it, build your own ritual around whatever phase you feel most called to (see page 63). I keep a notebook with my New Moon intentions and check in with it at the Full Moon. At the Dark Moon, I take an extra salty cleansing bath with lavender essential oil.

NEW MOON   WAXING CRESCENT   FIRST QUARTER MOON   WAXING GIBBOUS

Simple Actions for Each Moon Cycle

Before we get to the right ritual for you (see page 63), let's look at how to best use each moon phase and the simple actions you can take at each one.

NEW MOON

Use it for: Setting intentions and calling something in for the cycle/month ahead. The intention that you choose will be your main focus throughout the rest of the phases. No pressure though! You can adjust and edit that intention—in fact, the moon encourages that.

SIMPLE ACTION: TURN INWARD

Take some time to ground yourself and get into your body. Try focusing on your breathing, doing gentle movement like stretching or dancing, or soaking in the bath. Ask yourself what you most need and take enough time and space to listen. Take note of the very first thing you hear—it will likely be something simple.

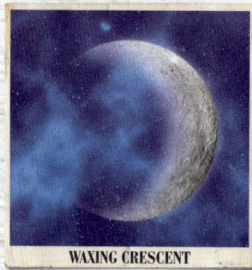

WAXING CRESCENT

Use it for: Feeling into your intention. Relax and see how your intention feels in your life right now.

SIMPLE ACTION: GIVE YOURSELF SPACE

I'm talking mental space. Make time for a little meditation at this time and allow yourself to just be without actively pursuing your intention. You can also give yourself physical space by getting into nature and doing a walking meditation. While you're walking, focus on your body—your feet, your legs, your lungs—before moving on to the environment around you. Just notice what you see and feel.

FIRST QUARTER MOON

Use it for: Following that momentum you're feeling. During this time you may want to reach out and connect with someone who might need your help or just benefit from a kind word.

SIMPLE ACTION: TAKE A BABY STEP

Take an action out in the world that's reflective of your intention. For example, if you're trying to call more love into your life, text a friend to express what you love about her. Or more abundance? Make a donation to a cause that you really care about, or volunteer your time.

WAXING GIBBOUS

Use it for: Looking back on the time that's passed since the New Moon and reflecting on how you're feeling about it.

SIMPLE ACTION: TAKE NOTE

Take the next few days to observe how you're feeling and how it might line up (or not) with your intention. Sum up your feelings in a few words and put them in your calendar, planner, or journal.

FULL MOON

WANING GIBBOUS

LAST QUARTER MOON

WANING MOON OR BALSAMIC MOON

FULL MOON

Use it for: Celebrating the cycle so far, everything that you've worked on, and everything you're releasing. A celebration can be something small like an intentional meal or a gathering with friends.

SIMPLE ACTION: RELEASE

Let out any pent-up energy or emotions by sharing your experiences with others—perhaps in person with story medicine (see page 64). You can also dance, do breathwork (see page 113), take a salt bath, or cry. Crying *in* a salt bath is major release medicine.

WANING GIBBOUS

Use it for: Observe what's naturally shifting in your life. How does it feel to release and let go a little bit? It's okay to grieve whatever it is you released.

SIMPLE ACTION: RECHARGE

Do what you've gotta do to take good care of yourself. Sleep is the biggest and best thing you can do for recharging your mind and body—let yourself get into bed early or don't set your alarm for the following morning. Sleep as much as you need or can without guilt. If you have trouble sleeping, give CBD a whirl (see page 100) or make a calming infusion (see pages 106–107).

LAST QUARTER MOON

Use it for: Examining your boundaries. How are you shedding the things you don't need? What does that look like for you? Do you need to put a new system in place to help yourself?

SIMPLE ACTION: SAY NO

If there's an obligation, something, or someone that you keep saying yes to but your heart's not in it, try saying no. It can just be this one time or going forward. Say no to an invitation that feels "meh" or an opportunity that just doesn't sit right with you. Flex your no muscle.

WANING MOON OR BALSAMIC MOON

Use it for: Feeling your feelings. I often feel physically drained around this time. Knowing this helps me be kinder to myself and anticipate the need for more gentleness.

SIMPLE ACTION: REFLECT WITH GRATITUDE

Spend some time with yourself to consider the highs and lows of this past cycle and do a little gratitude practice. Make a list in a journal or a voice memo on your phone of all the things you're grateful for. Finally, ask yourself what you need—it's often the simplest things like water, a rest on the couch, or a big baked sweet potato—and give it to yourself.

Creating the right ritual for you: The New Moon Tune-In

Tuning in is about temporarily clearing away distractions and bringing your focus inward. This ritual can take as little as 10 minutes or as long as an hour, and be as simple or elaborate as you like—whatever works best for you.

1. Put your phone on airplane mode or turn it off.
2. Find a space where you feel comfy and cozy and you won't be disturbed.
3. Take a few deep breaths before you begin.
4. Have something to write with (I think writing things down with a pen and paper solidifies magic.)

A high-vibe New Moon ceremony

The following are suggestions only. Ultimately, do what feels good to you. Don't worry about feeling silly or weird. If a part of you wants to do it, give it a try.

Pick a playlist of songs: Choose songs that set the right mood. Get classy with some Mozart or channel your sexiness with some vintage French music.

Cleanse your space: Burn Palo Santo or rosemary (see page 44 for more smoke-cleansing ideas.)

Get your mood lighting on: Candles, salt lamps, and twinkle lights are all encouraged.

Involve essential oils: Pick a scent for the mood you're looking to evoke—some suggestions are lavender for peaceful calm, sweet orange for positivity, rosemary for focus, rose for a little extra love.

Grab your Tarot deck: If you're stumped about what you really need to call in at the moment, you can always consult the deck (see Chapter 6).

Move your body: Take a walk, dance, or do yoga to get into your body and de-clutter your mind.

Run a bath: Add some Epsom salts.

Make a special tonic: Choose any tonic, tea, or elixir that feels delicious and nourishing to you.

HOW TO DO IT

Prepare your space with your chosen ambiance enhancers and do your favorite body-relaxing practice. Sit down and take a few deep breaths. Ask yourself what you'd like to invite in or how you'd like to feel. Note the first responses you get. Focus on an intention rather than a goal. Goals are great and can work in tandem with intentions, but intentions focus more on the mental, emotional, and spiritual, rather than the physical. State your intention in the present tense out loud and write it down. End by grounding yourself with a meal or drink and slowly enjoy it. Some examples of intentions might be, I intend to...

☆ Slow down
☆ Find joy in the everyday
☆ Follow my intuitive hits
☆ Go on an adventure once a week
☆ Be more intentional with my time
☆ Soften
☆ Move only in ways that feel good
☆ Meditate, dance, or cook daily
☆ Express love
☆ Do what feels cozy

The Full Moon check-in and release

Within two short weeks of the New Moon, it will be time to check in at the Full Moon, get serious about what's not working, and release it. Some questions you can ask yourself:

☆ What's holding me back from fully stepping into my intention?

☆ What feels stuck?

☆ What feels like a roadblock?

☆ What insecurity is rearing its head?

WRITE AND RELEASE

Think about these questions seriously—journaling always helps here, and letting yourself write it out can help the wise voice of the intuition flow more easily.

And the releasing? This is the fun part. Burning is popular for its visceral, finite destruction of a scrap of paper. Write out what you're releasing on a paper, read those things out loud, and throw it into a flame. I've done this in a firepit and with a candle over my kitchen sink—both work! You can also rip it up and flush it down the toilet or dissolve it in water. You can then physically move the energy out of your body by dancing or shouting—or both. Turn a song up loud that captures the moment and go for it. Seriously go wild.

STORY MEDICINE

Coming together as a community to be seen and heard is a potent ways of releasing. Radical Awakenings, an online community run by Alexandra Roxo, encourages local covens to get together at the Full Moon for Story Medicine. This is about holding a safe space for others, in which anyone can share a story and/or what they are releasing. There's something alchemical about in-person gatherings that can heighten the magic of letting our thoughts, emotions, and words leave our bodies.

HOSTING A STORY MEDICINE CIRCLE

Gather your witches together: This can be one or two trusted friends or open it up to others via social media.

Pick a theme: Center the stories around the theme.

Let one person talk at a time: Set a time limit per person and appoint someone to keep time. Let everyone talk, if possible. When it's your turn, open yourself up to the support of others."

Don't allow responses: No one is to respond to the story with words, sounds, or nodding. Everyone should listen neutrally without judgment.

Acknowledge the speaker: When they're finished, say thank you, smile, or place a hand on your heart.

Afterward: Listen to music and enjoy something grounding to eat.

Tarot Reflections

Card 1: How can the current moon phase help me?

Card 2: What was the lesson of the last moon cycle?

Card 3: Where can I focus my intention at this time?

See page 11 for guidance.

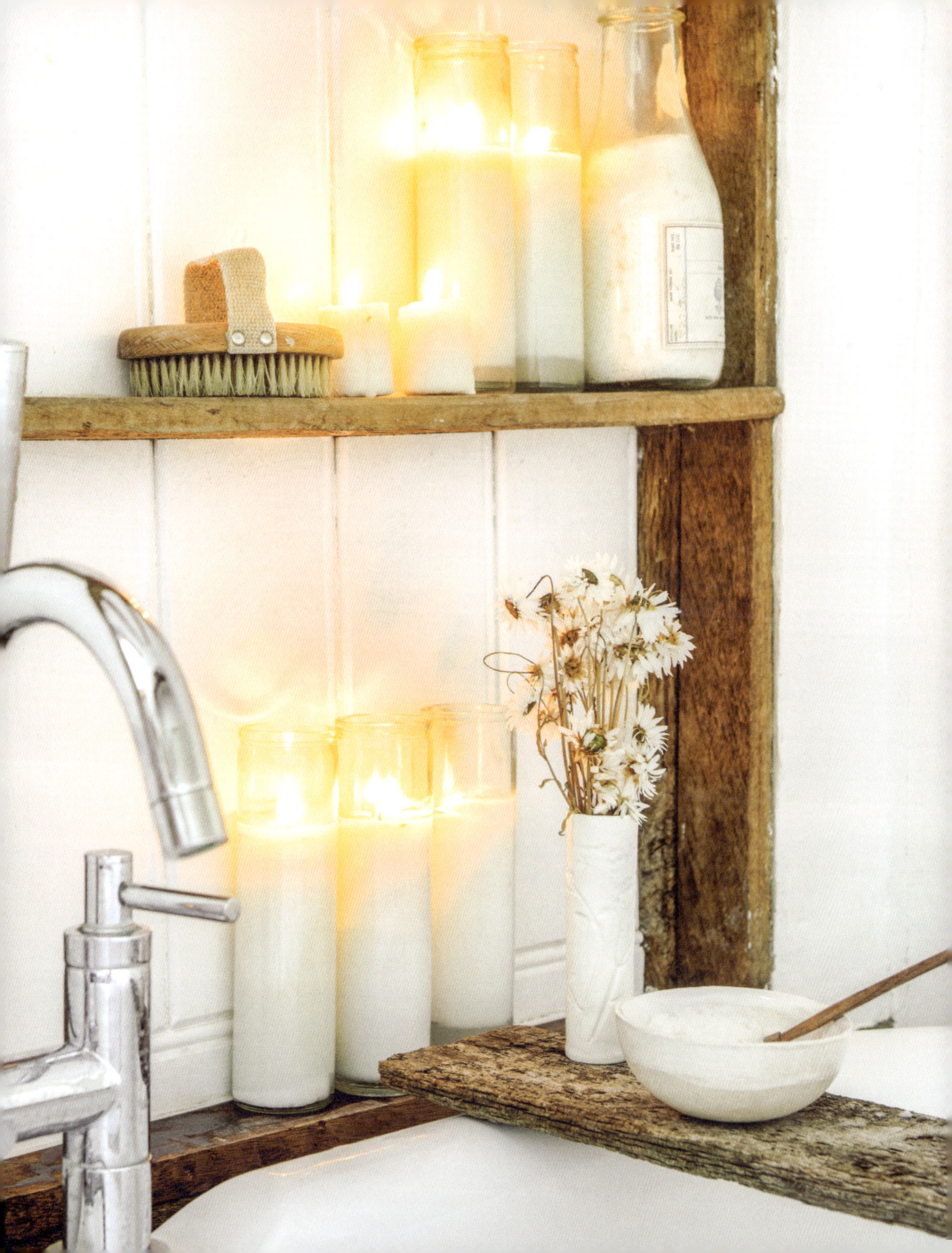

Full Moon pasta feast

I love the idea of gathering witches together on the Full Moon. The Full Moon is a celebration time, which to me calls for pasta. Pasta is great base for almost all seasonal produce, so check what's in peak season at each Full Moon and go from there. Think fresh or slow-roasted tomatoes and zucchini/ courgettes in summer, squash and broccoli in the fall, Brussels sprouts and kale in the winter, and greens, asparagus, and peas in the spring.

I love mixing up the type of pasta I use, too. There are so many great gluten-free and alternative flour pastas out there—some of my favorites are chickpea, brown rice, black rice, spelt (contains gluten), and quinoa pasta.

Roasted Cauliflower Pasta

This cauliflower pasta is a great template and you can swap in other roasted veggies in its place. Serve with a simple shaved fennel or arugula/rocket salad to make it a full dinner.

Serves 4

- ☆ 1 large head of cauliflower, cut into bite-sized florets
- ☆ freshly squeezed juice of ½ lemon, divided
- ☆ 1lb/450g dried pasta shape of your choice (I love cavatelli or shells)
- ☆ ¼ cup/60ml olive oil, plus extra for roasting the cauliflower
- ☆ 3 garlic cloves, finely chopped
- ☆ ½ teaspoon red pepper/chilli flakes
- ☆ ½ cup/35g grated Parmesan, plus extra to serve
- ☆ fresh flat-leaf parsley, finely chopped
- ☆ ½ cup /50g walnuts, toasted and roughly chopped
- ☆ salt and freshly ground black pepper

Preheat the oven to 400°F/200°C/Gas 6.

Place the cauliflower florets in a bowl and toss with a generous drizzle of olive oil and sprinkle of salt, then spread out on a baking tray. Bake in the preheated oven for 30–35 minutes until golden brown. Remove from the oven and spritz with half the lemon juice, tossing to coat. Set aside (this step can be done ahead if you wish).

Put a big pot of water on to boil for the pasta. Once the water is boiling, add a big dose of salt followed by the pasta and cook for a minute or two short of the package instructions—usually about 7–10 minutes, depending on the pasta (you want it to be al dente— with a little bite to it, not too mushy).

Meanwhile, heat the olive oil in a large skillet/frying pan (preferably one with high sides) over a medium-low heat. Add the garlic and cook, stirring, for 1 minute, then add the red pepper/chilli flakes and set aside.

Once the pasta is cooked, drain it, reserving a cup of pasta water, and transfer back into the pasta pot. Add the garlic-chilli oil. Stir in the cauliflower, followed by the Parmesan, a pinch of salt, and some freshly ground pepper. Add the rest of the lemon juice and a splash or two of pasta water (a few tablespoons at a time, adding more as needed) and stir—this is so the pasta doesn't get too gluey with the melted Parmesan.

Top with fresh parsley and toasted walnuts and serve in bowls with additional cracked black pepper and Parmesan.

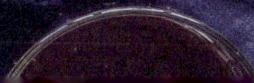

Chapter 5

Self-awareness with Astrology

Do you ever feel like a contradiction of yourself? Or wonder why you keep on attracting the same kinds of relationships or work scenarios? The answer could lie in your birth chart—a visual interpretation of the sky the moment you were born.

We're made up of much more than the one zodiac sign you might be familiar with (this is usually your sun sign), and your birth chart can help show you the connections and complexities that are completely unique to you.

As a Leo Sun and Cancer Rising, I have often felt like the usual descriptions of my sun sign didn't apply to me. Because Leo is ruled by the sun and Cancer by the moon, the energies are opposed, creating a more complicated picture than any magazine horoscope could touch on. And this doesn't even skim the surface of all of the aspects that go into a chart.

Astrology offers a more in-depth perspective on others and yourself. Learning someone's sun sign—and hopefully their moon and rising signs—is a fun and fascinating way to cut to the core of who someone might be and how they express that in the world. Even if they don't "believe" in it.

Gain Insight with Astrology

Astrology is the study of the way the cosmos affects us as individuals on Earth. Where the Earth is in relation to constellations of stars (these are the zodiac signs) and the planets in our solar system impacts the energies at play at any given time.

Astrology is thought to be roughly 2,000 years old (although some sources claim it's as much as 10,000). It was the first form of the study of the stars and celestial bodies and was long considered a respected science until astronomy became the standard, but the two are closely linked.

Today, astrology is a beautiful blend of science, intuitive interpretation, and personal insight. It can guide us through the cycles of the year and of our lives, through external relationships and the relationship we have with ourselves. Astrology isn't necessarily a belief system, but a tool for self-examination and acceptance. It can help us get to know ourselves on a new level if we use it for self-knowledge and self-care.

Astrology isn't going to tell you what to do or what's going to happen in any certain terms, but it can show you the energies at play and guide you on your path. Ultimately, you have free will as a human being on this planet. There is plenty of information written in the stars, but it's what you choose to do with that information and energy that counts.

By learning your own personal astrology through your birth chart (see page 74), you can reach a better understanding of your core essence and get another perspective on how to best take care of yourself. Learning about the major aspects of your chart can show you how to work with, instead of against, the unique energies present within you.

Astrology can help you live your most authentic expression through having awareness and compassion for yourself and your unique abilities.

The Signs

I've pulled together a list of the zodiac signs and their super-powers, shadows, and a few other defining traits. This isn't an exhaustive look at each of the signs, but a helpful overview.

Every sign has things that they're notorious for—these tend to be the imbalanced or shadow aspects of the signs. But there is also the more balanced, higher expression of every sign that can be considered the strengths or super-powers. I've included both. See page 72 for an explanation of the elements and qualities.

♈ ARIES Mar 21–Apr 19

Element: Fire
Quality: Cardinal
Super-Powers: Independent, excited, initiative, leadership, entrepreneurial, inspiring, direct, decisive, trailblazer
Shadows: Hot-headed, reckless, selfish
Ruling Planet: Mars

♉ TAURUS Apr 20–May 20

Element: Earth
Quality: Fixed
Super-Powers: Self-worth, groundedness, the senses/sensual, dependable, deliberate, pleasure, sustainability, stability, generous
Shadows: Stubborn, overindulgent, self-doubt
Ruling Planet: Venus

♊ GEMINI May 21–June 20

Element: Air

Quality: Mutable

Super-Powers: Social, intelligent, expressive, connectors, story tellers, multifaceted, learning and teaching, witty, versatile

Shadows: Duplicitous, gossip, unreliable

Ruling Planet: Mercury

♋ CANCER June 21–July 22

Element: Water

Quality: Cardinal

Super-Powers:: Intuitive, empathetic, receptive, nurturing, creating a home, supportive, unconditional love, gentle

Shadows: Moody, suspicious, closed off, defensive, mommy issues/insecurity

Ruling Planet: Moon

♌ LEO July 23–Aug 22

Element: Fire

Quality: Fixed

Super-Powers: Loving, heart-centered, warmth, creativity, playful, passionate, self-expression, courageous, giving

Shadows: Self-centered, attention-seeking, dramatic

Ruling Planet: Sun

♍ VIRGO Aug 23–Sept 22

Element: Earth

Quality: Mutable

Super-Powers: Organized, hard working, healer, thoughtful, attention to detail, discerning, improving, good habits

Shadows: Perfectionistic, judgmental, uptight

Ruling Planet: Mercury

♎ LIBRA Sept 23–Oct 22

Element: Air
Quality: Cardinal
Super-Powers: Beautifying, balance, harmony, social, artistic, objectivity, diplomacy, ideas, considerate, romantic
Shadows: Codependent, dishonesty, indecision
Ruling Planet: Venus

♏ SCORPIO Oct 23–Nov 21

Element: Water
Quality: Fixed
Super-Powers: Deep connection, magnetic, brave, magical, powerful, transformative, passionate, intensity
Shadows: Obsessive, controlling, secretive
Ruling Planet: Mars and Pluto

♐ SAGITTARIUS Nov 22–Dec 21

Element: Fire
Quality: Mutable
Super-Powers: Joyful, explorer, big ideas, search for meaning, philosopher, honest, optimistic
Shadows: Restless, overzealous, blunt
Ruling Planet: Jupiter

♑ CAPRICORN Dec 22–Jan 19

Element: Earth
Quality: Cardinal
Super-Powers: Reliable, integrity, structure, determined, powerful, achiever, impactful, building something that serves others, creating a harmonious family
Shadows: Rigid, workaholic, harsh, daddy issues
Ruling Planet: Saturn

♒ AQUARIUS Jan 20–Feb 18

Element: Air
Quality: Fixed
Super-Powers: Innovative, visionary, hopeful, progressive, collective improvement, revolutionary, individual, equality, technology
Shadows: Aloof, extreme, self-righteous
Ruling Planet: Uranus and Saturn

♓ PISCES Feb 18–Mar 20

Element: Water
Quality: Mutable
Super-Powers: Empathy, deep wisdom, spiritual, psychic, imaginative, adaptable, uplifting, compassionate
Shadows: Escapist, martyr, can dissolve into relationships, isolationist
Ruling Planet: Neptune

ELEMENTS

Fire: Creative energy, spark, confidence, essence, action, straightforward, putting yourself out there, masculine/Yang
Water: Emotions, feelings, psychic abilities, intuition, our inner world, flow, alignment, release, receiving, healing, dreams, feminine/Yin
Air: Thoughts, brain chemistry, mental and social connection, communication, language, stories, ideas, core beliefs/the stories we tell ourselves, masculine/Yang
Earth: Self-worth, the body, purpose, abundance, work, groundedness, refining, security, pragmatic, the senses, feminine/Yin

QUALITIES

Cardinal: The beginning of a season, initiatory energy, the leaders, excitement, creativity, dynamic movement
Fixed: The middle or height of a season, stabilizing energy, the makers, powerful, persistent, resistant to change
Mutable: The end of a season, flexible energy, the chameleons, easily adaptable, wise, comfortable with change

HOUSES

The houses represent areas of life. The planets and the signs that are contained within the houses are the aspects of ourselves that we embody in these areas of our lives.

There are 12 houses of the zodiac and each is ruled by one of the signs (known as the natural ruler), which can help you figure out the meaning of the house. Unless you're an Aries rising, your houses will typically not be ruled by the natural rulers.

First (natural ruler: Aries): Self, identity, style
Second (natural ruler: Taurus): Worth, security, possessions
Third (natural ruler: Gemini): Communication, education, siblings
Fourth (natural ruler: Cancer): Home, family, roots, inner self
Fifth (natural ruler: Leo): Creative expression, pleasure, children
Sixth (natural ruler: Virgo): Rituals, health, routines, work
Seventh (natural ruler: Libra): Partnership, marriage, shadow self
Eighth (natural ruler: Scorpio): Healing, renewal, sex, death, inheritance
Ninth (natural ruler: Sagittarius): Philosophy, adventure, teachers
Tenth (natural ruler: Capricorn): Responsibility, recognition, career
Eleventh (natural ruler: Aquarius): Community, groups of friends, hopes, goals
Twelfth (natural ruler: Pisces): Spirituality, subconscious, psychic abilities, escapism

For example, you could have your 11th House in Taurus, meaning that your community and friendships are built up over time and tend to be long-lasting (maybe you've maintained the same close group since high school). You might enjoy hosting lavish dinners for friends filled with good food, music, and ambiance.

PLANETS

The planets represent different parts of our personality. They can look different depending on the sign and house they show up in in your chart.

Mars: Motivation, action, assertion, sexuality

Venus: Self-worth, love, abundance, values, attraction

Mercury: Communication, thoughts, intellect

Saturn: Lessons, structure, accountability, ambition

Jupiter: Surprises, expansion, abundance, search for meaning

Uranus: Revolution, change, inspiration, uniqueness

Neptune: Dreams, spirituality, healing, unconditional love

Pluto: Transformation, life and death cycle, surrender

Moon: Intuition, emotions, internal world, needs

Sun: Expression, being seen, truth, the Self

Your Birth Chart

Your birth or natal chart is a map of where the stars and planets were in the sky at the exact moment of your birth. It's a map of where you've been, what energies will play out in your life, and how you'll relate to challenges. I often hear the birth chart described as a blueprint of your soul or who you are—your strengths, weaknesses, and the potential you possess.

I love thinking about it as a guide or key to how we can become our highest selves. It shows us how we can shine, express, evolve, and find contentment. Seeing a professional astrologer is a great way to get the full picture. See page 139 for some of my favorites.

Getting to know your birth chart

The three biggest aspects of your birth chart are your Sun, Moon, and Rising signs. The Sun sign is what people usually read their horoscope for. (But your rising sign horoscope can be more relevant to you!)

☉ SUN SIGN

What it is: The Sun is what sign or season of the zodiac the Earth was moving through at the time of your birth. It changes every month.

What it means: Your Sun is how you shine, the authentic expression of yourself, your identity and inner focus.

Reflection: How can I come back to my core self in the present moment?

AC RISING/ASCENDANT SIGN

What it is: The sign on the horizon the moment you were born. It changes every couple of hours.

What it means: How you're seen by others, first impressions, how you show up day-to-day and the outer shell you present. Related to the Shadow and the Soul's purpose, and what you're here to cultivate. It's the key to your soul self.

Reflection: What balance do I need to cultivate?

☽ MOON SIGN

What it is: The sign the moon was in the moment you were born. It changes approximately every two-and-a-half days.

What it means: Your emotional nature, instinctual behaviors and reactions, safety, the unconscious. It's how you find comfort and contentment. Look to the moon for self-care.

Reflection: How do I nourish myself?

How these three work together

Our Rising Sign is kind of a big deal. It determines the house system in our chart, with the rising/ascendant line of our charts marking where the first house begins. It shows us what we're here to learn about, to embrace more, and to balance out. If you can embrace your Rising Sign, it will steer you toward your purpose. If your Sun and Rising signs can work together and you can work to embody balanced versions of each, you'll be able to find your flow and encounter less resistance. The Moon Sign supports you on this journey to your purpose and freedom. I think of her as a guide for parenting yourself on your path to working with your shadow self (see Chapter 9) and unbalanced aspects. She's here to comfort you, but also give you the medicine you need.

JUMP IN: **Look up your birth chart**

To look up your birth chart, you'll need your birth date, time, and location and an internet connection. Unfortunately, if you don't have your birth time and location, you won't be able to get an accurate chart with your Rising Sign but you can still find your Sun Sign and get an estimated chart.

Plug this information into a website like Astro.com, which will draw you a free chart. You'll get a circular diagram, like the one below, divided into pie-like slices with a bunch of symbols, numbers, and lines. The chart is made up of three main systems working together to create a complex web of information that's unique to you. The three systems include:

★ 12 Signs

★ 12 Houses

★ 10 Planets (Sun and Moon are counted as planets)

Once you get your birth chart, identify your Sun, Moon, and Rising signs. What's your first reaction to these, given what you know about each? Does anything really make sense or are you resistant to one or all of these aspects? Think about how these three things relate to one another and to you personally.

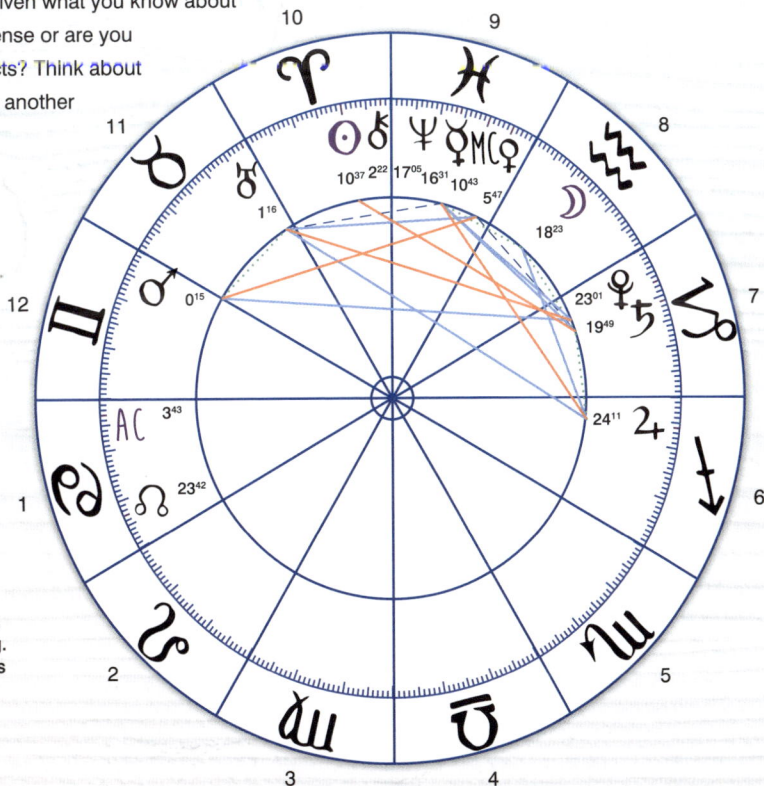

This birth chart shows an Aries Sun, Aquarius Moon and a Cancer Rising. The lines drawn between the planets shed light on how they interact.

Creating the right ritual for you: Moon Sign Self-care

The moon reflects our emotional body and internal world. It helps us feel comforted, safe, and content, making our individual moon sign a great guide for self-care.

Really good self-care is individual and specific to you. That being said, there are a few simple things that I think we can *all* benefit from regardless of our astrology:

☆ Some form of meditation

☆ Screen-free time

☆ Getting outside, preferably near trees or bodies of water

Below is a list, by moon sign, of ideas for feeling comforted, balanced, and restored. But if anything on the below list calls to you go for it—no matter what your moon sign is. Listen to your intuition and do what you're drawn to. **Note:** Many of these self-care practices are covered throughout this book so I haven't explained them in detail below.

Aries Moon

Needs: Freedom, expression, movement, energetic release, steadiness.

Try: Candle magic, dancing, going on an adventure to a new neighborhood, physical exercise (running, hiking), sex magic, a cooling face mask, scalp massage.

Reflection question: How do you connect to your wildness? What helps you stay grounded?

Taurus Moon

Needs: Nature, connecting to the body, sensual pleasures, luxury, predictability.

Try: Creating a morning routine, cooking a meal using a few of your favorite ingredients, long walks outside, walking barefoot in the grass, cleansing your home (clutter clearing and/or vibe clearing), intimate time with yourself or a partner, getting a massage.

Reflection question: Does your routine include something that connects you to the Earth and your body? How does your environment impact your mood?

Gemini Moon

Needs: Good conversation, socializing, grounding, calming the mind.

Try: Group exercise, journaling/stream of consciousness writing, reading a novel, story medicine, focused breathing or breathwork, EFT tapping, finding a few essential oils you love, working with your hands—knitting, baking, crafting.

Reflection question: How do you calm your mind? Can you get to a quiet enough place to let your intuition be heard?

Cancer Moon

Needs: Alone time or time with the people closest to you, time at home, mood release, communicating feelings and emotions.

Try: Cooking nourishing meals for yourself and/or friends and family, meal prepping, cleansing your home, spending time near the ocean or water, crying it out, taking a salt bath, inner child and shadow work, embodiment breathing, EFT tapping, reiki.

Reflection question: Are you taking time to nurture yourself (as opposed to just nurturing others)? What does nourishment look/feel like to you?

Leo Moon

Needs: Creative expression, affection, play, affirmation.
Try: Dancing, a daily dressing ritual (what makes you feel like a Queen? Most like yourself?), creating a meal without a recipe, making art, writing what's on your mind, or taking photos. Getting out in the fresh air to exercise, having heart-centered conversations, offering your time for someone in need (can be a friend or organization), body work, Tarot journaling.
Reflection question: Can you find ways to express yourself daily? Are there ways you can do it that you might not automatically think of?

Virgo Moon

Needs: Purpose, organizing, analyzing feelings, to shut off.
Try: Clutter clearing, journaling, Epsom salt bath, sleeping, cleansing your workspace, acts of service, making a green smoothie, guided meditation, making a gratitude and/or accomplishment list, going on a solo hike, tending to plants, cognitive behavioral therapy.
Reflection question: What gives you a feeling of purpose or satisfaction that's not necessarily work-related? Can you make more time for this?

Libra Moon

Needs: Peace, beauty, art, equal relationships.
Try: Meditation, altar building, painting, house magic, feng shui, writing poetry or stories, making an at-home honey face mask (à la Cleopatra), yoga, buying yourself flowers, spending quality time with friends and your love, hitting up a museum or gallery.
Reflection question: What do you feel like you're not getting enough of in your life right now? Can you find a way to make room for it and call it in?

Scorpio Moon

Needs: Inner exploration, transformation, empowerment, release.

Try: Breathwork, meditation, shadow work, Tarot, keeping a dream journal, sex magic, kundalini breathing or breathwork, eating dark chocolate, fire or candle magic, acupuncture, gratitude practice.

Reflection question: What's your biggest shadow right now? What would it feel like to own it and embrace it?

Sagittarius Moon

Needs: Adventure, nature, travel, philosophical conversation.

Try: Outdoor sports, yoga, traveling, local adventure, getting to the beach or woods, learning something new, acting on intuition, hosting a circle for story medicine.

Reflection question: When do you feel the most free? Can you find a balanced way for freedom to be a part of your everyday life?

Capricorn Moon

Needs: Family, structure, heart opening, levity.

Try: Music, comedy, breathwork, creating a manifestation list, doing a heart opening meditation or breathing exercise, getting a massage, stream of consciousness journaling, stretching, orgasm.

Reflection question: Are there ways you can be nicer to and ease up on yourself? Can you open up to others in a small way today?

Aquarius Moon

Needs: Community, creative work, a cause, expression, rebellion.

Try: Reading Tarot for yourself, a grounding practice (barefoot walking, time outside, or embodiment breathing), volunteering your time, organizing a story medicine group or full moon gathering, giving yourself a free afternoon to adventure somewhere or do whatever you think of at the time.

Reflection question: Do you feel like you have a good community around you? What does a good balance of support and freedom look like to you?

Pisces Moon

Needs: Time by water, spirituality, grounding, strong sense of self-worth.

Try: Embodiment practices like dancing, breathwork, or hip circles; taking photos, painting, drawing, loving kindness meditation, cleaning out your closet, crying, reiki, sleeping, going to a sound bath or finding some meditation music you vibe with, jumping on a trampoline, shadow work, a daily gratitude practice, saying no.

Reflection question: How do you communicate your needs to others? Is there a way that you can do this that feels both empowering and easeful?

Tarot Reflections

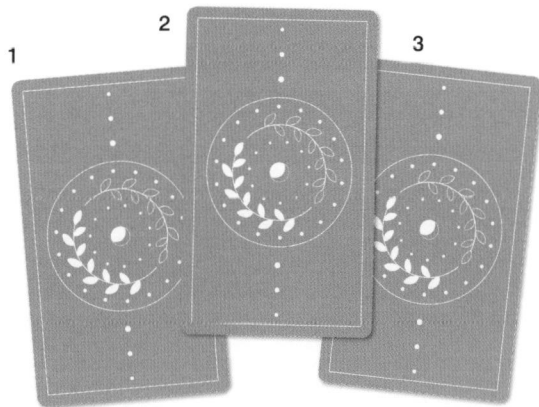

Card 1: What can I learn from the tensions or difficult aspects of my chart in this phase of my life?

Card 2: What's my release valve for these tense aspects?

Card 3: How can I practice self-acceptance?

See page 11 for guidance.

Heart-Opening Reishi Hot Cacao

Reishi is an adaptogenic mushroom known as the queen healer or the mushroom of immortality and is said to reduce stress, promote the body-mind-spirit connection, and enhance emotional balance. Paired with heart-opening cacao, this twist on hot chocolate is the ultimate companion for diving deep into your birth chart and journaling on what you find. Cacao is said to help connect you to your higher self, balance your masculine and feminine energies, and improve clarity around purpose.

Cacao Laboratory (see page 139) makes my favorite blends of ceremonial cacaos with four flavors—each corresponding to the elements—Earth, Air, Fire, Water.

Makes 1 cup

- ☆ 1 cup/250ml boiling water
- ☆ 1 tablespoon cacao powder or ceremonial cacao
- ☆ 1 date or 2 teaspoons maple syrup
- ☆ 1 tablespoon collagen powder (optional)
- ☆ 1 heaped teaspoon coconut butter
- ☆ 1 teaspoon coconut oil
- ☆ ¼ teaspoon reishi mushroom powder
- ☆ sprinkle of cinnamon
- ☆ pinch of sea salt

Combine the hot water with the rest of the ingredients in a blender and blend at high speed until smooth and frothy. Pour into a mug and serve hot.

II

THE HIGH PRIESTESS

Chapter 6

Connect to Your Wisdom with Tarot

Forget what you think you know about fortune-telling and "scary" insights, Tarot cards are best used to get in touch with your intuition. They are a tool for getting clear on where we are in our lives and what we're experiencing. Using the cards as an intuitive self-care practice isn't about predicting the future, but about seeing the energies currently at play and getting real about how we can best move forward.

Tarot decks have been around in some form for centuries. Most likely their first iteration debuted in the Middle Ages, but the messages of the cards and the journey of the Tarot deck have evolved to reflect universal human experience. Today there are many decks with different artwork and themes to express an even wider range of understanding. At the heart of every deck, though, is the potential you possess. We're all creators of our own reality and the cards can show us hints to light the way to a path that's best for us, but they in no way determine our fate.

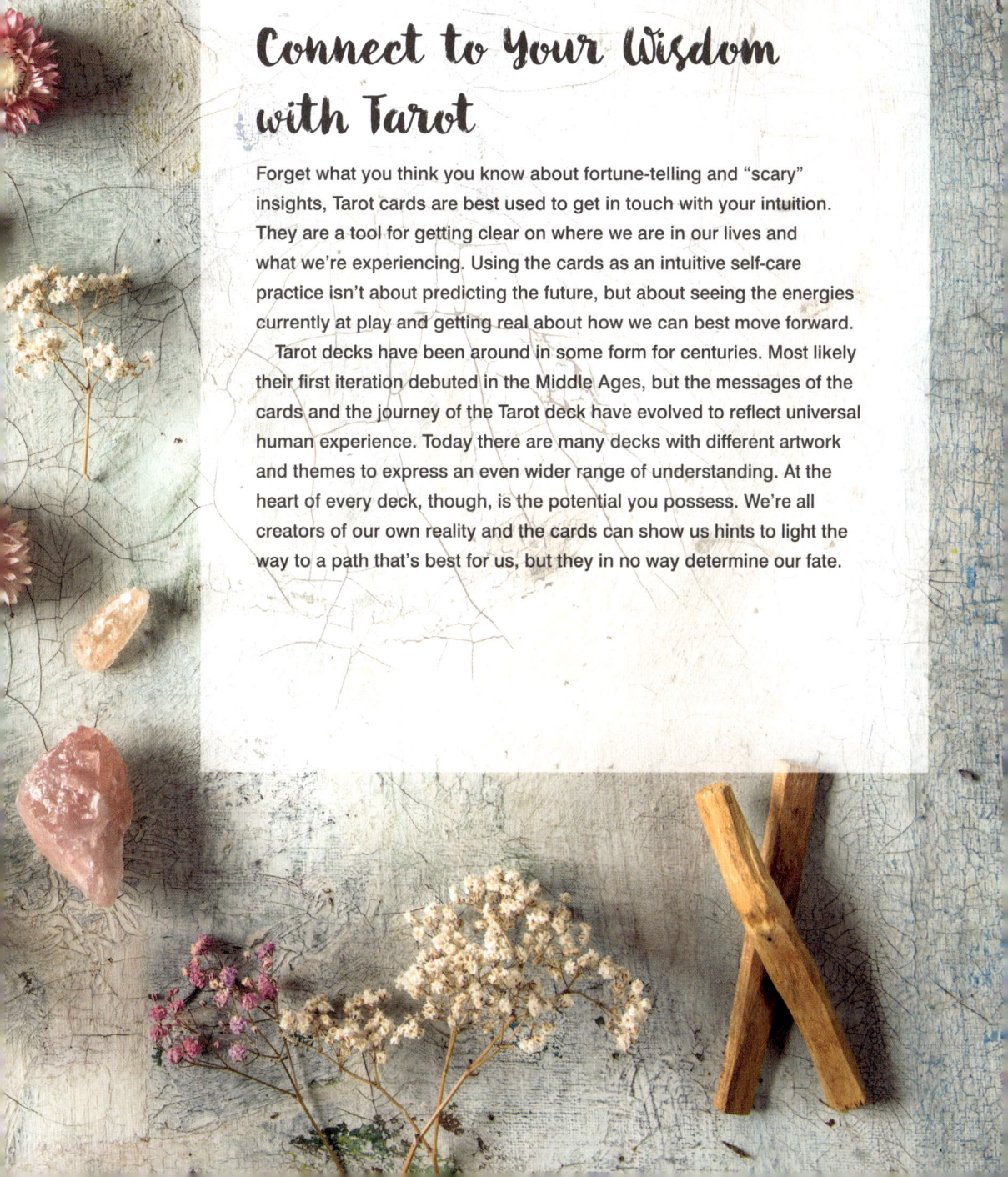

About Tarot Cards

Each Tarot deck has 78 cards, made up of the Major Arcana and Minor Arcana. The 22 Major Arcana cards are, well, *major* life themes, phases, and shifts. The 56 Minor Arcana cards are made up of suits—very similar to a typical playing card deck.

The suits are typically wands, swords, cups, and pentacles. These suits represent the four elements—wands are fire, swords are air, cups are water, and pentacles are earth. The numbered ace through 10 cards reflect everyday occurrences, nuggets of knowledge, and feelings. The court cards (pages, knights, queens, and kings) often come up as aspects of our personality or archetypes that we most need to focus on or call upon.

All the cards correspond to instances—both big and small—in our lives. These themes are universal truths of the human experience. We can use the cards to get in touch with what's really going on with us and to help us reflect on what we're learning and how to deal with the situation at hand.

Intuition and Tarot

One of the questions that often comes up around this witchy work is: How do you know when your intuition is talking to you? And how can you hear it more clearly? While I'm all about using your breath and body to tune into your intuition, sometimes we need extra tools to help bridge the gap between mind and intuition. The cards are a great visual tool that can help you paint a fuller picture of what intuition is trying to communicate.

The Tarot can nudge us to look at something from a new perspective and suggest positive actions to move through what's happening for us right now. Most often, it reflects back to us where we are and helps us identify what we can't fully articulate.

Why work with the Tarot?

Learning the Tarot and journaling with it has been one of the most (if not *the* most) life-changing practices I've added to my self-care arsenal. I've found that it helps me easily access my intuition, examine underlying issues that are fueling my anxiety, and find gentle ways to use this information to feel better and ultimately grow as a person.

Since I started my Tarot journaling practice, I've learned a ton about the cards, their history, and many of their different meanings. It's taught me about self-care more than any of the other tools in this book. It's taught me that sometimes self-care looks like not taking any action at all. Or like getting serious about my boundaries. Or just going out with my friends and celebrating. You might find that using the Tarot helps you feel more grounded, expansive, connected, intuitive, or all of the above. It will put you in touch with a deeper part of yourself—to connect you to the magic you already possess as the badass you are. In the pages that follow I share some of the big things it's taught me.

JUMP IN: **Choose a deck**

Go out and buy your own deck. You don't have to wait until someone gifts one to you, as some lore suggests. Do some research, look at images, and see what stands out to you. If you can, handle the deck in-person at a store to really get a feel for it. Try out different decks—it may take you a few tries to find your deck. But enjoy the process of discovering what it is. The Smith-Waite is a standard deck with medieval fairy tale-like imagery and is great for learning on, as many contemporary decks are based on it—but it's very white and binary. Other popular decks include The Wild Unknown, The Aquarian, and The Starseed and Moonchild decks—but this isn't even close to all that's available.

You are always growing and learning

The Tarot itself is a circular, spiraling journey. We are constantly working through the archetypes and energies illustrated in the deck. The meanings of each card can shift and expand over time, as our relationship with, and understanding of, the deck evolves. We will keep coming back to a card from different angles, learning new lessons from it each time. And that's kind of how life is—sometimes we feel like we're back-sliding because we keep dealing with the same negative thought pattern or having the same issue with a partner, but if we're practicing awareness, each time we find ourselves there we know more than we did last time.

There is endless reading, learning, and interacting you can do with the Tarot. As someone who is happiest when I'm learning, I find this comforting. I know I'll never consider myself a master of the Tarot because being a student of it is far more fun and interesting.

Your intuition knows stuff

Using Tarot cards as a tool for self-inquiry and self-awareness is really what it's all about. While it can help us tap into the energy within and around us and make sense of it, the intuition is what's running the show. The intuition directs us toward certain cards and uses them to help our mind make the right connections.

The Tarot has taught me how to embrace this intuitive side of myself and honor it. And while it's not always easy to hear it clearly, especially after decades of not being aware of it or ignoring it, Tarot is here to help us access it. So listen to it, dive deeper if something is unclear, and work with it—it won't steer you wrong.

If you're always hoping for "positive/everything-is-great" cards, you're missing the point. All of the cards hold valuable lessons, but we have to be ready to go further with the message. When someone draws a card like The Devil or Death card, the initial response may be to panic or reject it. But a better way to work with a challenging card is to ask, "What's this bringing up for me? Why don't I want to look at what's coming up?"

These cards can be strong catalysts for positive change in your life if you're willing to take the time to examine what they bring up for you and how to move forward with a new sense of awareness.

Good versus bad is unhelpful

Much like hoping for "positive" cards, I don't like to put any of the cards into the bad or good camp. The scariest-looking cards can have the most welcome messages, if you're willing to see them outside of a binary. As with all these lessons, this is as useful in Tarot as it is in day-to-day life. Sometimes we just don't have the scope and distance from something to be able to determine if something is for our greater potential. Often something that feels like a big loss at the time (perhaps missing out on a job or breaking up with someone) is putting you on the path to something bigger and better.

There is always action you can take

Confidence comes from taking action and the Tarot always has advice on what action to take. The actions the Tarot will suggest may not look as straightforward as you might want, but there is always something you can do to bring you back into balance or give you the encouragement you need. Sometimes it's taking a breath, going outside, or letting yourself cry.

Everything is happening for you, not to you

The Tarot really exemplifies this idea that even though things might seem chaotic on the surface, there's a greater lesson and growth that can happen as a result. Instead of seeing things as setbacks, delays, or failures, try viewing everything that's happened thus far and what will happen as a way of setting you on the right path.

We're here to learn about ourselves, and to contribute in a positive way. The Tarot can help us see situations for what they are and for the possibilities they offer. Most paths aren't linear and aren't meant to be. Try to embrace where you're at and the complicated way you got here.

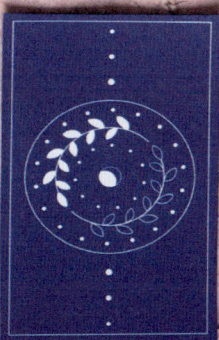

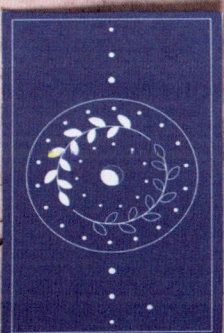

Using the Tarot for Self-care

In this chapter I want to show you how to use the Tarot as a personal practice for getting in tune with your intuition, which will help you learn the Tarot as you go, too. For getting to grips with the card meanings and all things Tarot, there are great resources available (see page 139).

Starting a Tarot practice is a way of befriending and being tender with yourself. When we regularly use the cards to connect with what's happening in our day-to-day lives, we're checking in with ourselves, which is the first step in self-care. One of my Tarot teachers, Anna Toonk, says, "When you're learning or getting a practice solidified it's helpful to treat it like an experiment or like you're a Tarot detective. Take the data in, record it, observe and be really open. Tarot is such a good way to bust up goal-oriented type-A perfectionism tendencies. It's so humbling and empowering to be okay with being a student and sort of floundering. You just have to dive in. You will be wrong, and that's okay!"

The best way that I've found to fully process the lessons of the Tarot is by journaling. Doing this daily has taught me a lot about taking an honest but non-judgmental approach to self-reflection and about the cards themselves. It helps you dive deep into the card meanings, connecting them to your own experiences, and forming a relationship with them. Sure, a relationship with cards may sound ridiculous, but it's a real and important part of learning how to read Tarot and for using it for your mental, emotional, and physical wellness.

Daily Tarot practice for self-care

For this practice, you'll need a Tarot deck, journal, pen, and a little quiet time. Before you begin working with the cards you might want to meditate, or just take a few deep breaths to drop into the present moment and yourself. See page 91 for ways to create the right Tarot ritual for you.

Start by pulling one card a day to keep it simple and get to know the cards. Set aside 15 minutes each day to check in with your deck. You can make it a part of your morning coffee routine or in the evening when you're winding down for the day.

1. SHUFFLE AND ASK

Hold your cards for a moment and then begin to shuffle. Think about what you'd like to know as you're shuffling. The way you shuffle doesn't matter—just get those cards nice and mixed up. Stop shuffling when you feel it's right and your question is fully in your mind.

If you don't know what to ask, start with a simple: What do I need to know today? Avoid yes or no questions or queries about the specific timing of events as you likely won't get a clear answer. The Tarot works best when you're looking into a situation more deeply to find out what's lying below the surface, what motivations are there, and what's available to help you make the situation better. The cards won't make choices for you, but can help empower you to make the best decision for yourself.

Other types of questions you might ask:

☆ What's going on for me right now?

☆ How can I work through this feeling I have right now? Or, How can I unblock myself from x feeling?

☆ What's going to be useful to me in this situation?

☆ How might I feel if I decide to (fill in the blank)?

☆ What strength will help me with this situation?

☆ What energy would be the most helpful for me to embody right now?

Setting yourself up for the day:

☆ How can I get into the flow today?

☆ What does alignment look like for me today?

☆ What part of me wants to shine right now?

For blah days:

☆ What belief is at the root of this discomfort?

☆ What's my main block in this moment?

☆ What expectations am I holding on to?

☆ What do I need to release for my evolution?

2. DRAW YOUR CARD AND LOOK AT IT

I mean really look at it. What feelings do you get as soon as you look at it and hold it in your hand? Does the image remind you of anything? Does the card seem to carry a strong emotion to you? How might it relate to your question? What clues are in the imagery that you notice only the second or third time you scan the image?

Jot down the first few things that pop into your head about the card and how it corresponds to your question. This is where we really start flexing that intuition muscle!

3. CHECK WITH THE EXPERTS (OPTIONAL)

I believe that your intuition is the ultimate authority here, especially because this journaling exercise is all about you getting in touch with you. So if you're on a roll with Step 2 on the previous page, keep going and skip this if you don't feel the need.

But if you want to learn the cards, I suggest checking with a source that resonates with you. Personally, I hated the little booklet that came with my Smith-Waite Centennial deck and didn't find that any of the descriptions landed with me. I threw it out in favor of a few resources I return to regularly (see page 83).

4. WRITE IT OUT

Write everything down—all your gut reactions and any meaningful descriptions you find in your outside research. As you write, what questions come up for you? Are there any actions you feel would be useful now that you have this insight?

Now's the time to get really real with yourself. Try to get to the root of what this card is highlighting for you. If it makes you slightly uncomfortable, take it as a good sign—that's where the growth potential is! Often once you start writing, more insights can present themselves to you. Write as much or as little as you need. It's interesting to have a record to refer back to later, too.

I know writing doesn't work well for everyone, but try journaling and see what comes up for you. If you find you work through things by saying them out loud, try recording voice memos on your phone instead. Listen back at the end of the day to see if your perception on something has shifted or been confirmed.

REPEATING CARDS

Repeating cards happen often in the Tarot, and for me, pulling the Queen of Pentacles four days in a row was the first sign that magic was really happening here. Cards that come up a few days in a row or within the same week or month are here to make us pay attention. It's how we know it's time to go deeper, open our eyes and heart, and maybe put a few more cards on the table to expand on what's going on. Repeating cards can happen for a couple of reasons:

1. **We're not fully grasping the lesson:** get curious, go deeper into the meanings, and meditate with it to work out what the card is trying to bring to your attention.
2. **We're in a time of mastery:** one of my teachers, Lindsay Mack, would say that the card is a gentle reminder that you're working through an expression of this energy and doing the deep work with it.

REVERSALS

Card reversals (when you pull the card upside down) can be useful when you're trying to tap into the energy of a card and how it relates to your experience. Often they make for a more interesting viewpoint of the cards. Reversals can mean many things, but a few ways of interpreting them that I come back to regularly are:

Go internal: Even if this card has an external vibe, the reversal is telling us to do the work within ourselves first, before working on what's external to us.

Look at something in a different way: We might not be available to the energy of the card at this time or just aren't feeling it. It's showing up because we need to take a closer look at it and why it's not landing with us. Seek out a new way to do something or a new approach.

Release: You could be in the process of moving out of this energy, it's showing up in a less-intense way, or you're being asked to release something that's blocking you.

Ask the deck for more clues if you're having trouble interpreting the reversal.

Tarot Spreads

There are plenty of intricate Tarot spreads you can do and a lot of books will map them out for you. I find that three-card spreads can be very helpful, so that's what I do most often.

A few of my favorite simple spreads

ANXIETY SPREAD (INSPIRED BY THE TEACHINGS OF LINDSAY MACK)

Card 1: What am I feeling right now?

Card 2: What's the reality of the situation?

Card 3: What's the best way to move forward today?

RELEASE SPREAD

Card 1: Where am I at right now?

Card 2: What expectations am I holding onto?

Card 3: What do I need to release?

GUIDANCE SPREAD

Card 1: How do I want to feel?

Card 2: What will get me closer to that feeling?

Card 3: How can I show up for myself right now?

MIND BODY SPIRIT SPREAD

Card 1: What does my mind need today?

Card 2: What does my body need today?

Card 3: What does my spirit need today?

NEW MOON SPREAD

Card 1: What lessons have I learned in this past cycle?

Card 2: What am I being invited to focus on in this cycle?

Card 3: How can I find alignment in this cycle?

Creating the right Tarot ritual for you

Part of reading Tarot involves tuning in and opening yourself up to the wisdom of the deck. This can be done in myriad ways, and ultimately comes down to what feels right to you.

Start by creating the right environment for yourself. This can include: alone time, making your favorite tea or coffee, lighting candles, burning incense or diffusing essential oils, saging or Palo Santo-ing your space, gathering a crystal or two, etc. After you spend some time with your deck, you'll know what feels right.

Shuffle in any way you'd like and tune into yourself using your breath to guide you. You can call in any guides, angels, or deities you feel drawn to or ask the universe to help you out.

Use any of the questions or spreads in this chapter to get you started. The important thing is being open. Press pause on judgments—against yourself or what you think other people will think of you—and come into the present moment. Any way you can do that will create the right ritual for you.

Creating your own Tarot spreads

While a predetermined spread is a great place to start, some of the best and most effective spreads are the ones you create yourself. I have a list on my phone of spreads that pop into my head while I'm out for walks or listening to a podcast. I'll come back to them later when I have a few quiet minutes and my deck.

Write down your main question and create a three- to five-card spread around that question and what might help you work through the situation or feeling. Then pick up your deck, shuffle, and draw cards accordingly, focusing intently on each individual query as you go.

Tarot Reflections

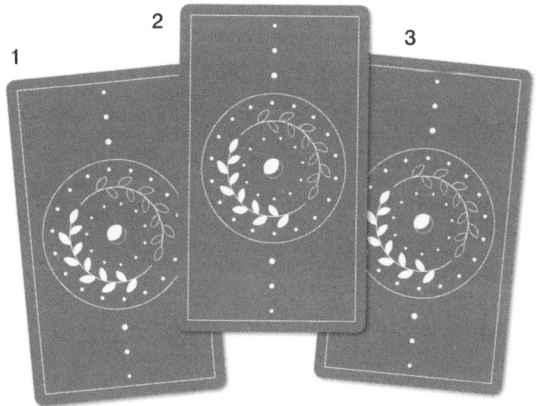

Card 1: What kind of work am I meant to do with this deck?

Card 2: Which card is my teacher right now?

Card 3: How can I go deeper with this card?

See page 11 for guidance.

The Empress Breakfast

Channel your inner Empress for the first meal of the day. Ruled by Venus, The Empress is all about abundance, receiving, openness, and creativity—the archetypal feminine or Yin energy. Her symbols often include pomegranates (for fertility), wheat (for abundance of the harvest), and luxurious, natural surrounds. She rules all things we love and appreciate, therefore an Empress Breakfast is required to be delicious, beautiful, and a little fancy.

Serves 2

☆ olive oil, for greasing
☆ 1 small delicata squash, cut in half lengthwise, seeds removed, sliced into ½-inch/1-cm thick crescents, unpeeled
☆ sea salt
☆ 2 slices sourdough bread
☆ ½-cup/100g fresh ricotta cheese
☆ fresh basil, cilantro/coriander, or mint
☆ 1–2 tablespoons pomegranate seeds

Preheat the oven to 375ºF/190ºC/Gas 5.

Lightly oil a baking tray and spread the squash slices on it. Sprinkle with salt and roast in the preheated oven for 20 minutes. Remove from oven, flip the squash pieces, and return to the oven for another 10 minutes until tender. This can be done a day or two ahead, storing the squash in the fridge in an airtight container. Bring to room temperature or lightly reheat before using. You'll have extra to add to more toast or to salads and sides.

To serve, toast the sourdough. Spread ricotta on each slice and top with the squash, fresh herbs, and pomegranate seeds. Sprinkle with sea salt and drizzle with a little olive oil and enjoy immediately.

Chapter 7

Herbs & Plant Medicine for Wellbeing

Plants are magic. The leaves, roots, flowers, and fungi found in nature can provide a multitude of benefits for the human body. Everyday herbs contain potent healing properties for a wide variety of ailments and can help us manage stress and anxiety, boost our focus and mood, and recenter ourselves. They can also enhance our magic and intentions with their individual energy. Whether you cook with herbs and spices, create your own infusions or lattes, or simply buy some herbal tea or a CBD oil, there are many ways you can work with plant medicine and include it in daily rituals to improve your wellbeing.

Plant medicine is sometimes a term used to describe the intense, mind-altering experiences caused by taking plants like ayahuasca, psilocybin, peyote, and others. I don't explore these in this book, because I don't have personal experience with them. I believe that all plants—especially ones we consume regularly—have medicine for us.

As someone who has spent years as a food writer, recipe developer, and cook, plant medicine holds a special place in my heart. Once I began cooking mainly vegetarian and plant-based meals in my early 20s, I quickly felt the effects that plants have on my body and mind. Eating high-vibrational foods like plants and herbs helps us to connect the physical, mental, and spiritual, because what we eat becomes a part of us on every level.

Once I learned that foods (mainly the plant-based, found-in-nature, whole kinds) have both medicinal and magical benefits, I was beyond excited for the possibilities. Creating intentional meals and drinks that contain physical and metaphysical medicine can open us up to a whole new experience in the kitchen. Combining herbs and plants as a way to cull stress, feel more focused, or open up to self-love has become *the* ritual, one that I do every day in some form, even if I skip all the others.

The Power of Plants and Herbs

From the nourishment they provide the body and mind, to the magical properties they contain, plants and herbs have the power to change us on a cellular level. Even the gentlest chamomile tea or basil pesto has the potential to create a shift in our body.

Cooking with plants and herbs, steeping or planting them, using them to adorn your home or altar, or anything else you can dream up, can all be forms of magic, because plants themselves are magical. We can use plants to reinforce how we want to feel by incorporating types that match the energy we're looking to cultivate. Enjoy herbs and edible plants as part of your rituals to reinforce your magic or use them to create elixirs that are magic on their own.

Kitchen witchery

Kitchen witchery (see page 47) can be used to enhance your cooking experience and the meals you create. You can infuse meals, drinks, and treats with intention and positive energy. Herbs and plant medicine are a big part of kitchen witchery too, providing nutrients, healing, and mood-boosting effects, and support for your intentions with their magical properties.

Garden magic

Enhance your kitchen magic by growing your own culinary herbs on a windowsill or in a garden. Try growing rosemary, thyme, sage, chives, mint, or basil. Plants you've nurtured have an even more powerful force because your personal care is imbued in them—they taste better and are super affordable, too. Fresh and dried herbs aren't usually expensive, but seeds and soil are even cheaper given how much you get back from them.

As you use your herbs to marinate, steep, or garnish with, think about all the sun, water, soil, and care it took to get them here—they're an expression of love and strength.

Guide to Magical Plants

All plants contain magic, but the following is a beginner's guide to get you thinking about the possibilities of using herbs, flowers, mushrooms, and more in daily rituals.

Common herbs for all kinds of magic

Opposite and overleaf is a collection of common herbs and a few you might not have heard of. Most should be easy to find at grocery stores, herbalism shops, or online (see resources on page 140). Once you dip a toe into herbalism, you might find that you want to start your own mini herbal apothecary. It sounds silly, but when you begin learning about herbs, buying dried leaves, flowers, and seeds can become addictive. Start small and add to your collection as you learn more. Please use organic, responsibly sourced herbs if possible.

The energetics of plants reach far beyond just our physical bodies, they can alter our emotional and spiritual sides too. I have included just a few uses for each herb—both conventional uses as well as magical applications, which are often complementary. I invite you to do further research before ingesting an herb to make sure it's right for you at this time. For more information, check the resources at the back of this book.

BASIL/SWEET BASIL
Uses: Inflammation, blood-cleansing, nausea, anxiety, depression
Magical applications: Abundance, wealth, love, empathy

CHAMOMILE
Uses: Insomnia, digestion, irritability, restlessness, colds
Magical applications: Peace, meditation, purification

CILANTRO/CORIANDER
Uses: Headache, digestion, inflammation, nausea, detoxifying, skin health
Magical applications: Love, health, healing

CINNAMON
Uses: Inflammation, digestion, circulation, toothache, cold/flu and infections, regulates blood sugar
Magical applications: Warmth, lust, spirituality, psychic powers, healing, success

DAMIANA
Uses: Tension, anxiety, boosts mood and relaxation
Magical applications: Aphrodisiac, love, visions

DANDELION
Uses: Liver health, healthy gut flora, hormone health
Magical applications: Divination, wishes, psychic powers

ELDERFLOWER
Uses: Antiviral, immunity boosting, cold/flu
Magical applications: Protection, healing, sleep, prosperity

FENNEL SEEDS

Uses: Digestion, cramps, lactation

Magical applications: Healing, confidence, protection

GINGER

Uses: Cold/flu, nausea, cramps, inflammation, migraines, infections, stimulating the systems of the body

Magical applications: Success, power, money, love

HIBISCUS FLOWER

Uses: Healthy blood pressure, boosts heart health and circulation, reduces fluid retention

Magical applications: Openness, pleasure, sensuality, beauty, divination

LAVENDER

Uses: Tension, anxiety, poor sleep, headaches, depression, bacterial or fungal infections, bug bites

Magical applications: Calm, peace, longevity, happiness, love, protection

LEMON BALM

Uses: Stress, nervousness, anxiety, sleep, mood boosting, relaxing

Magical applications: Healing, love, friendship, success, soul soothing

MUGWORT

Uses: Liver tonic, healthy circulation, stomach issues, irregular periods

Magical applications: Strength, spirituality, dreams, healing, psychic powers, calling in the goddess Artemis

NETTLE

Uses: Fatigue, allergies, eczema, weak hair, skin and bones, aids lactation and boosts metabolism

Magical applications: Protection, nourishment, healing

OAT TOPS OR OAT STRAW

Uses: Bone health, depression, stress, mood stabilizing, nervous system soother

Magical applications: Prosperity, fertility

PARSLEY

Uses: Digestion, heart health, kidney stones, irregular periods, antioxidants

Magical applications: Protection, fertility, shadow work

PASSIONFLOWER

Uses: Anxiety, insomnia, calming, focus

Magical applications: Peace, sleep, friendship

PEPPERMINT

Uses: Stomach issues, nervousness, headaches, tense muscles, relieves itching and inflammation, memory and alertness, cold and fever

Magical applications: Focus, healing, purification, psychic powers, travel, presence

RASPBERRY LEAF

Uses: Women's health, fertility, tones uterus, eases cramps, preps body for birth
Magical applications: Protection, soothing, love, pain relief

RED CLOVER

Uses: Hormone balancing; heart, blood and lung health; cough, fever
Magical applications: Banishing negative spirits, lust, success

ROSE

Uses: Pain, depression, heart health, inflammation, bladder infections
Magical applications: Heart opening, healing, luck, love, emotions, prophetic dreams

ROSEMARY

Uses: Boosts cognition; antioxidants; skin protection; heart, digestive and liver health; improves mood; anxiety
Magical applications: Healing, sleep, care, mental ability, youth, purification

SAGE

Uses: Memory and attention, infections, sore throat, hot flashes, sore muscles, improves insulin resistance
Magical applications: Longevity, wisdom, immortality, wishes

SCULLCAP

Uses: Anxiety, insomnia, inflammation
Magical applications: Peace, love, fidelity, stops circular thinking

THYME

Uses: Infections, cold/flu symptoms, fungal infections, wounds, digestive and menstrual cramps, inflammation
Magical applications: Bravery, strength, good dreams, new beginnings

TURMERIC

Uses: Inflammation, muscle and joint pain, liver health, eczema, insulin resistance
Magical applications: Purification, protection

VALERIAN

Uses: Insomnia, anxiety, stress, calming the nervous system
Magical applications: Sleep, deep relaxation, self acceptance, ending guilt

Adaptogens and mushrooms

An adaptogen is a root, herb, or fungus that regulates the stress response in the body. As their name suggests, they adapt to what your particular body needs, making them a good aid for varying stress levels and bringing our bodies back to homeostasis. They work best when taken daily over an extended period of time.

ASHWAGANDHA
What: Root
Uses: Fatigue, reproductive health, insomnia, longevity, stress, anxiety boosting energy and libido

CHAGA
What: Mushroom
Uses: Liver health, immune health, cancer-inhibiting properties

HOLY BASIL (TULSI)
What: Leaves and flower
Uses: Brain fog, anxiety, stress, pain relief, immune system support, promotes good circulation, aids meditation and promotes compassion

MACA
What: Root
Uses: Hormone balancing, reproductive health, memory and cognition, energy

REISHI
What: Mushroom
Uses: Fatigue, inflammation, immune system support, heart health, antioxidants

Flower essences

Flower essences are different from herbal tinctures and essential oils in that they focus specifically on emotional healing (like releasing emotional blocks or promoting confidence). The distillation of different types of flowers in an alcohol or vegetable glycerin base creates tinctures that are meant to alter the way we feel about ourselves in certain ways. The vibrations of the flowers have strong healing properties, so you only need a few drops throughout the day.

I've found flower essences to have a beautiful impact on my emotions and mood—and there's seemingly a type of flower for each challenge or change you seek. I took Red Chestnut for unnecessary worry during my pregnancy, Crab Apple Blossom to break my addiction to perfectionism, and Alexis Smart's Ganesh blend, which helped me stop doubting myself enough to write this book. See resources, page 140.

CBD

CBD, or cannabidiol, is another potent form of plant medicine. Made from the hemp plant, this supplement usually comes in an oil-based tincture. CBD can be helpful for Issues like anxiety, depression, insomnia, chronic pain, inflammation, and more. A whole plant CBD oil contains cannabinoids, among other naturally occurring chemicals, that have anti-inflammatory effects and protect the nervous system.

CBD comes from the cannabis plant but the difference between CBD and marijuana is the amount of THC (tetrahydrocannabinol), the chemical component that has psychoactive effects. CBD will only contain trace amounts of the stuff (less than 0.3 percent), so it won't get you high.

CBD is a gentle form of plant medicine that can help reset the body and nervous system. You can incorporate CBD into your daily rituals by taking it as a supplement under the tongue or by adding it to tonics, infusions, smoothies, or meals. See resources, page 140.

JUMP IN: **Working with herbs**

Dried herbs last longer than fresh and are easy to store, but fresh herbs are amazing and just as useful. A mix of both will help you use what's in season, what you have in your pantry, and add more flavor to anything you make.

Cook (fresh or dried herbs): Use herbs to enhance the flavor and health benefits of a meal. Blend, chop, sprinkle, or sauté them. Leafy herbs are better for adding to dishes right before serving and woody or dried herbs and spices should be added to hot oil or butter at the beginning of cooking to bring out the best flavors.

Tea and infusions (fresh or dried herbs): The difference between a tea and an infusion is that tea is steeped for a shorter amount of time (usually around 10 minutes), whereas an infusion is steeped for

longer, making it stronger. I prefer an infusion to get the most flavor and benefits from an herb.

I typically make infusions with dried herbs (see page 106), but if you have fresh herbs like mint or basil, you can let them steep in room-temperature or cold water for a cooling, lighter kind of infusion. This is great in the summertime when we often have a lot of these herbs.

Baths (fresh or dried herbs): Add infusions to your bath to let your skin soak in the benefits. Put together blends of herbs to restore your energetic body and combine with a cup of Epsom salts for an ultra relaxing experience. Or make a 4-cup/1 litre infusion as directed on page 106 and add it to your bath.

You can also add fresh herbs to a warm bath if you're willing to do the cleanup. Try a sprig of rosemary for a grounding, cleansing bath or rose

petals (ideally from your own garden and not sprayed with chemicals) for heart-soothing.

Tincture (dried herbs): Tinctures are concentrated herbal supplements made by steeping herbs in alcohol or vinegar for an extended period of time (the general rule is a month). These are very powerful and only require a few drops either in a drink or directly into your mouth.

Powders (dried herbs): Herb and superfood powders can be expensive, but it's easy and much more cost-effective to make your own. Blitz your herb of choice in a high-speed blender or coffee grinder until it's in powder form, then store in an airtight container. Add herb powders to smoothies, tonics, and coffees. Nettle powder is amazing as a nutrient-dense "green superfood" powder for smoothies. Chamomile powder can be blended with coffee to balance out a hectic morning. Start by adding ½ teaspoon of powder for a single serving.

Blend (fresh herbs): Add fresh herbs to smoothies, sauces, soups, or pestos. Leafy green herbs are best for this. Try adding a handful or two of parsley, mint, or basil to a green smoothie or make a multi-herb pesto with 2 packed cups/40g of herbs, ½ cup/60g toasted cashews, ½ cup/120ml olive oil, juice of half a lemon, and salt to taste.

What Does Your Body Need?

Tuning into your body and figuring out what it needs is a great practice to cultivate. This will open the line of communication between your mind and intuition and help you care for yourself in the best ways possible. Once you figure out what your physical, emotional, and spiritual needs are, you can start to play with different combinations of food, herbs, or intentions to support you.

Start by asking yourself: What am I craving? Is this in any way related to what you're craving spiritually? If you can spend time with a craving and think about what it means to you, you may find a more holistic way to enjoy that food. And I don't mean holistic in the sense of finding a "healthier" option, but a way of enjoying the ritual of eating that's satisfying on all levels.

So here's an example: You're craving pizza. All that melty cheese and sweet tomato sauce brings up feelings of comfort, nostalgia, and happy memories.

Can you eat your pizza with a loved one? Maybe play music that makes you remember a sweet memory or feeling while eating. Then sprinkle some fresh basil on your slice for a little abundance magic to bring in more good times in the future.

It can sound a little silly, but getting intentional with food, cravings, and what you cook can create real magic in your life. Not only will you enjoy the ritual of eating more, but you can use mealtimes and tea breaks to create more of what you want.

Creating the right ritual for you: Design Your Own Herbal Infusion

Plants can provide great support for any of the magical rituals we create for ourselves. Sometimes a guided meditation or breathwork session will bring up a lot of emotions and new insights and making your own infusion can help you ground down, recover, and reinforce the healing you're undergoing. Or you can make an infusion to accompany a Tarot journaling session or walk in the park to help you recenter and tune into your body.

Designing your own herbal infusion only takes a few minutes, but it can create really powerful shifts in your health and intentions. Just like we can identify food cravings, we can use our powers of self-knowledge to identify what we need energetically to create herbal combinations that uniquely benefit us.

1. Identify what you need on an emotional and physical level and set an intention for this infusion. It can be to feel soothed, more relaxed, energetic, or loving— whatever you want or need.

2. Assemble a few herbs that correspond to your needs. See the list of herbs on pages 97–99 and the recipes overleaf for some ideas.

3. Add herbs to a 4-cup/1-litre glass mason jar or heat-resistant container. I usually add about 1–2 tablespoons of each herb, adding more of the pleasant-tasting herbs. Do this mindfully by focusing on your intention for every spoonful of herbs you add.

4. Boil filtered water and let cool for a few minutes or add a bit of cold water to lower the temperature quickly. Fill the jar with water and gently stir the water and herbs together, then cover the jar to keep all the natural oils in. I don't like to add a tight-fitting jar lid just yet, as it can be hard to get off later.

5. Let the infusion steep for 2–8 hours on a countertop.

6. Strain out herbs and enjoy warm, at room temperature, or chilled. Mix half hot or cold water with half your infusion (the infusion will be strong).

7. (optional): Add lemon, lime, or sweetener of choice if desired.

Store strained infusions in clean glass jars in the fridge for up to 4 days.

Tarot Reflections

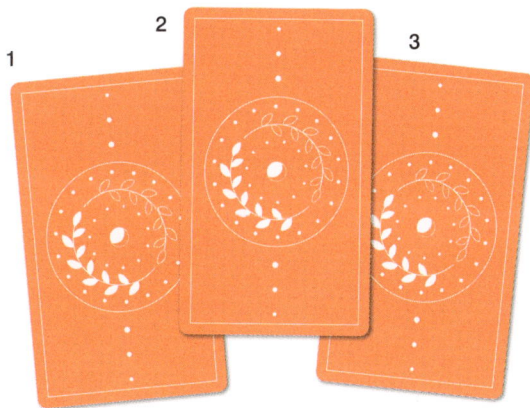

Card 1: What's true for me today?

Card 2: What does my body need?

Card 3: How can plants help me today?

See page 11 for guidance.

Infusion Recipes

Please note, all the infusions included here use dried herbs and flowers unless otherwise indicated. The quantities are intended for a 4-cup/1-litre infusion unless otherwise noted, and can be diluted with water to enjoy throughout the day. Feel free to play around with the proportions and what you have at home.

Hibiscus Chill-Out Iced Tea

This is one of my favorite summer teas. I serve it chilled and it feels cooling to both the body and mind.

☆ 3 tablespoons hibiscus flowers
☆ 2 tablespoons chamomile
☆ 1 tablespoon lemon balm
☆ freshly squeezed juice of 1 lemon
☆ honey or maple syrup to taste

Steep the herbs (see page 105). Once you've strained the herbs and returned the infusion to a clean glass jar, stir in the lemon juice and sweetener. Store in the fridge. Serve over ice by filling half the glass with the infusion, then topping up with filtered water.

Shavasana

For when you need that full-body calm at the end of the day. Helps with anxiety and daily stressors and soothes frayed nerves. The lavender is optional—it has strong calming properties, but I personally don't like to drink it (I prefer whiffing an essential oil instead). If you're into it, add away.

☆ 2 tablespoons chamomile
☆ 1 tablespoon passionflower
☆ 1 tablespoon skullcap
☆ 1 tablespoon oat straw or oat tops
☆ 1 teaspoon lavender (optional)

Steep the herbs (see page 105). Strain the herbs and enjoy the infusion warm or chilled, mixing one part hot water with one part infusion (the infusion will be strong) or one part cold water with one part infusion over ice.

Meditation Aid

A caffeine-free way to boost your brain power and tap into your personal genius. Sip as part of a meditation or throughout the workday.

- ☆ 2 tablespoons peppermint
- ☆ 2 tablespoons nettles
- ☆ 1 tablespoon holy basil

Steep the herbs (see page 105). Strain the herbs and enjoy the infusion warm or chilled, mixing one part hot water with one part infusion (the infusion will be strong) or one part cold water with one part infusion over ice.

Hormone Helper

A blend for nourishing the body and balancing hormones. I use sweet and mellow spearmint as a flavor enhancer for these verdant-tasting ingredients.

- ☆ 2 tablespoons spearmint
- ☆ 1 heaped tablespoon red clover
- ☆ 1 heaped tablespoon nettles
- ☆ 1 tablespoon oat straw or oat tops
- ☆ 1 tablespoon raspberry leaf

Steep the herbs (see page 105). Strain the herbs and enjoy the infusion warm or chilled, mixing one part hot water with one part infusion (the infusion will be strong) or one part cold water with one part infusion over ice.

Ginger, Lemon, and Honey Cold Buster

This tried and true combination eases cold symptoms and speeds healing. The recipe doesn't follow the same dried herb/steeping formula as the previous infusions and comes together much faster. I love to drink this even when I'm not sick, as a virgin hot toddy on a cold night or after eating a big meal (it's great for digestion, too).

- ☆ 1-inch/2.5-cm piece of fresh ginger, peeled and thinly sliced (I like to do this on a mandoline)
- ☆ 1½ cups/350ml just-boiled water
- ☆ freshly squeezed juice of ½ lemon
- ☆ 1 teaspoon raw honey
- ☆ pinch sea salt and pinch ground cayenne

Combine the ginger and boiling water and let steep for 15 minutes. Drain the liquid from the chunks of ginger or scoop them out and set aside. Add the lemon juice, honey, sea salt, and cayenne to the infusion, adding more hot water to bring the temperature up. Stir well.

Chapter 8

Healing with Energy Flow & Movement

Energy is the life force that courses through our bodies. It's known throughout cultures by many different things: qi, prana, the breath of life. When our energy is in balance, we're in homeostasis or at the point of balance that our body desires to maintain, but energy can become stuck in certain places, slow down, or be too intense due to factors like stress or trauma. To help nudge us back to our equilibrium, we must work with our energy to get it moving and flowing at the right speed. Taking some slow deep breaths, going for a walk, and doing a body scan meditation are all ways to move energy through our bodies.

The term energy work encompasses a lot of practices and rituals in this book. These are things that are meant to change us on a multidimensional level—physically, mentally, emotionally, and spiritually. Moving energy through our bodies using tools like breathwork, reiki, and tapping helps our energy to flow, touching on all of these levels as it does. The flow of energy promotes balance and homeostasis, and provides healing and a feeling of wholeness that our soul craves.

As with the embodiment practice at the beginning of this book (see page 23), these energetic practices serve to help us come back to ourselves and our bodies through simple and intentional actions. And while there are a ton of great classes, books, and practitioners out there specializing in things like reiki, breathwork, and yoga, I love that so many of these tools are free. You can move energy by walking, dancing, and breathing whenever or wherever you choose.

Change Through Energy Work

Whether we're experiencing stress, anxiety, sadness, anger, fatigue, pain—whatever—energy work can change our state of being. Energy work and movement alchemize our life force into something new by creating internal motion and flow where there were blocks. We have the power to create substantial shifts by using our bodies, breath, and voice and we can use these tools and practices to find moments of calm, joy, clarity, and love.

Healing is an ongoing process that we will never fully be done with, but there are layers we can shed as we go deeper within ourselves and get closer to the core self. These practices help us scrub away the layers that we don't need or want anymore. When we choose to engage with our breath and body on a regular basis, we clear the channel for magic to happen.

Acupuncture is probably one of the most well-known forms of energy work. Working with meridian points on the body, small, thin needles are inserted into specific points to allow for the qi, or energy, of the person to flow freely. Different points can be stimulated depending on the issues being experienced. Personally, I was amazed by how effective acupuncture was at recalibrating my hormones after coming off the birth control pill, easing muscle tension, and improving digestion. I don't include acupuncture in the energy work list in this chapter only because you can't do it on your own, but I suggest you give it a try if you're interested.

Energy work plays with the more subtle frequencies within us. Spanning from emotions to the nervous system, it has the capacity to change the way we operate on a moment-to-moment basis.

Sympathetic versus parasympathetic

The autonomic nervous system influences how we use the energy in our bodies and controls automatic responses like heart rate, digestion, arousal, and breathing. Part of energy work is about getting us back to neutral, which often involves switching from the sympathetic to the parasympathetic nervous system response. The sympathetic nervous system function is also known as the "fight or flight" response. It's the stress response we'd need if we were running from danger, so it's good for a high-intensity workout, but many of us are operating in this system all day long as a reaction to checking our inbox or commuting to work.

What we need more of is the parasympathetic response, or "rest and digest" mode, which lowers heart rate and tells our body it's safe to carry out functions like digestion and balancing hormones. The breath is a huge factor in signaling to our body that it's safe. If we can take steady breaths, with long exhales, we're able to shift out of an anxious or stressed-out state (which registers as fear) and communicate to the nervous system it's time to calm down. By using simple breathwork and mindfulness tools, we can take charge and change our physical and emotional response.

Movement versus exercise

I used to exercise. I would force myself to run through pain, depletion, and lack of rest until I started considering movement as an alternative. While they can look similar, movement is about establishing a real connection to my body, whereas exercise was a way to force my body to do something. After years of this forceful mindset, my body rebelled with injury and chronic pain. Now I simply move my body in ways that feel good. For me this mostly looks like stretching, walking, dancing, and at-home yoga.

Empowering, loving movement can look and feel different for everyone at different points in their lives. At one time, running felt like freedom and optimism, until it didn't. Here are a few guidelines for joyful movement:

★ If you dread doing something, stop doing it.

★ Move in a way that feels kind and loving, not from a place of punishment or deprivation.

★ Don't continue to do something that's painful. Some discomfort is normal for certain exercises, but real aches and pinching pains aren't—this is your body communicating with you.

★ Combine movement with intention. Set an intention for your movement to carry with you throughout. Boosting your energy, clearing your mind, and connecting to yourself are all great intentions.

★ If you're feeling stuck, have low energy, or feel blue simply go for a short walk outside if you're able to.

JUMP IN: **Try an energy work practice**

There are a few different types of energy work that you can practice by yourself, within a group or class, or one-on-one with a practitioner:

☆ Breathwork

☆ Reiki

☆ Tapping or Emotional Freedom Technique (EFT)

Within each of these modalities there are many different approaches—for example, in breathwork there's an intense, controlled breathing pattern versus a simple slow inhale and extended exhale. Try a few different types depending on your mood and individual needs. Most of these forms of energy work are free to try and I've listed resources on pages 139–140 for apps, teachers, websites, and books that can help.

Breathwork

Breathwork is simply breathing with intention. Also known in the yogic tradition as pranayama, it's about directing and controlling the breath to support meditative and body practices. Even more than food and water, breath is essential to keeping our bodies going. As such, it's often taken for granted or deemed too simple to really help, but it's one of the best foundational healing practices you can do. And it's the most versatile of all energy work, because you can access it anywhere at anytime.

There are many different types of breathwork to choose from. It can be done as part of a meditation or movement practice or on its own, and it can help in a pinch when you're feeling anxious, triggered in some way, or in need of an energy boost. It can also move stagnant emotions and be incredibly healing if harnessed in a particular way.

Some of the most eye-opening, healing experiences I've had have been in breathwork circles. Led by a trained breathwork healer (two of my favorites are Jordan Catherine Pagán and Erin Telford—both trained by David Elliott), these gatherings focus on an active and continuous loop of controlled breathing with two inhales through the mouth—one into the belly, one into the chest—and one exhale through the mouth.

These sessions are intense and put the "work" in breathwork. It's challenging to keep going for an extended period of time, especially when your body starts tingling and emotions begin to rise up. Our bodies aren't used to this much oxygen coming in at once and some really incredible things start to happen if you stick with it.

In the first breathwork circle I attended, my hands went completely numb and I freaked out. Turns out this is normal, but I had no idea what was going on. Luckily Jordan, who was leading the group, reassured me and held space for my worries and I was able to continue.

I cry every single time I show up and do this intense form of breathwork. I view this as a good thing because tears are a clear sign of moving and releasing emotions. Often I run the gamut of emotions in one session, from anger to grief to feeling completely blissed out. And for 10–20 minutes afterward, I feel high and what I can only describe as "floaty". Sounds a little nuts, I know. And you might have completely different reactions when you do it, but how amazing is it that we can experience such a kaleidoscope of life just by using our own breath? If you're willing to go there and accept the challenge of surrendering to whatever comes up, it's quite a journey.

Not all breathwork is this intense, though. It can be subtle, mellow, and a less emotional experience than the one I've described above, which makes it easier to do regularly and throughout a typical day. Sometimes just committing to taking three deep breaths can shift my mindset. Coming back to the breath can clear a path between the body, mind, and intuition if we do it regularly *and* with awareness and intention.

A few breathing techniques I love

Simple: Set a timer for 2 minutes. Inhale for 5 counts, and exhale for 5 counts. Repeat as needed. This technique is great for clearing mental chatter, slowing down, calming, and resetting.

The 4-7-8 breath: Start by breathing in for 4 counts, hold for 7, and exhale for 8. This slows down your heart rate, which calms the body while giving the mind something to focus on. Great for sleep and anxiety.

The loud exhale: Breathe into your belly for 4 counts and while exhaling, make any noises you want for as long as you want. It could be a heavy sigh, grunt, laugh, or "ughhh." This technique is great for release, frustration, anger.

Pro tip: You can do breathwork lying down, sitting up, or standing. If lying down, put a pillow under your knees to relieve any stress on the lower back.

Tapping

Tapping or Emotional Freedom Technique (EFT) works with acupressure points of the body. It combines tapping with the fingers on a specific set of points while saying statements out loud for the purpose of releasing blocked emotions and moving energy in the body.

What you say will be a combination of what you want to unblock or release, how it makes you feel, and why you're having issues with it, while consistently coming back to the statement: "But I deeply love, forgive, and accept myself."

I've tapped on everything from family issues, to feeling frustrated, to procrastinating, to not being able to feel proud of my work. In my experience, it feels like a subtle unblocking of stagnant energy. Sometimes you'll cry, yawn a lot, or feel your stomach rumble—these are all normal (and temporary) reactions, but are an outward manifestation of moving energy.

Pro tip: Drink plenty of water before and after to help the energy move through your system.

Reiki

Reiki is the practice of channeling healing energy through touch. Reiki can be done without touch by hovering the hands over the body, but I think if it feels safe for the other person, touch can be very beneficial. Like acupuncture or acupressure, reiki works with specific points on the body to address certain physical, mental, or emotional issues.

Reiki masters perform attunements on others looking to be initiated into reiki healing. These attunements can be powerful experiences and it's important to learn the correct ways to use reiki on others before offering your services as a healer, but we all have access to reiki energy. Reiki energy is healing and loving energy from the earth that has the power to shift energy within the physical and emotional body.

Try doing reiki on yourself. After a meditation, breathwork, or before sleep when your mind is calm, place your hands on your heart, hips, or back—wherever needs the most attention. Picture a clear white light coming through the crown of your head, down to your heart, and out through your hands for a few minutes or for as long as feels right.

Pro tip: Focus on whatever area of the physical or emotional body calls to you. You might not feel the shift immediately, but commit to a week of daily self-reiki and see how you feel.

Movement

Movement is a form of alchemy for our internal world. It can bring us into the present, help us get unstuck, create new emotional states, and change our outlook, mood, and sense of self by connecting us to our body and changing the flow of our energy. We can use movement to work through difficult emotions in a safe way. Think of it as a way to release or as a way of experiencing your feelings safely. Using movement to work through something like anger or frustration could look like using kickboxing moves to express aggression, sprinting to channel your frustrations, or blasting a song and dancing hard. Use it to get embodied, present, and out of your head.

Beneficial movement is whatever makes you feel good. As I mentioned earlier in this chapter, movement can look similar to exercise, but it's about approaching it from a place of connection, love, and intention.

Try a few minutes of the following and see how you feel:

☆ Hip circles
☆ Dancing
☆ Walking
☆ Yoga
☆ Stretching
☆ Running
☆ Weight-lifting

Adding mantra to movement

IntenSati is a workout created by Patricia Moreno that pairs a mix of heart-pumping movement with affirmations. Each set of moves is partnered with a positive affirmation, which you say out loud while doing the moves. I had the pleasure of doing intenSati on a retreat. At first I was uncomfortable and felt embarrassed shouting things like "Yes I can!". But the more I did it and the louder I got, the more transformational it became. The result of a 45-minute session was a buzzing, sweaty, joyful feeling.

If you can check out an intenSati class, I recommend it, but you can try this concept on your own. Pick out a couple of personal affirmations you'd like to work with and pair them with moves like squats, jumping jacks, or lunges.

Pro tip: Move in ways that excite you and feel good in your body regardless of what you think you "should" do.

Yoga

Yoga goes beyond just a typical vinyasa flow—it's a combination of breathing techniques, meditation, philosophy, spirituality, and asanas or positions. Yoga means union in Sanskrit and can be thought of as a way to find union between the body and the universe or between the self and the higher self.

For the purposes of this section, I'm talking about yoga as a movement and asana practice. I'm not an expert, but after having a dedicated home practice for many years, I know that getting the most out of my time on the mat requires a holistic approach. In order to really change my energy with yoga, I need to combine focused breath, movement and poses, and intention. Without one of those elements I speed through, stay in my head, and miss out on a relaxed and restorative post-practice experience.

There are different types of movement yoga, from Yin to Kundalini, for different intentions and speeds. Explore different types according to what you need on a given day. I recommend cultivating a home practice, which allows you to do it whenever, for as long as you'd like, and gives you the freedom to try new things.

What's great about yoga is that there's mindfulness built into the practice. All you need to change your energy—whether you spend 5 minutes doing a few downward dogs or an hour-long flow—is to consistently move with your breath and come back to your intention.

Pro tip: Yoga with Adriene (see page 140) is a great online resource with a big library of videos to guide you in your practice.

YOGA NIDRA

A type of lying down guided body scan meditation, yoga nidra helps us connect to all parts of our body, allowing us to sink deeper into relaxation and really tune in to ourselves. It's a way to meditate that's more earthy and sensational. If you're having trouble listening to your intuition, connecting to your core self, and working with shadow (see Chapter 9) and triggers, commit to a daily yoga nidra practice for two weeks.

Similar to guided visualization or hypnosis, in yoga nidra we dip into the subconscious mind while anchoring through the body, so it can be a great way to retrain the nervous system. It involves setting a San Culpa at the beginning and/or end of the practice, which serves as your intention. If done regularly, the San Culpa is a gentle way to work with our subconscious and shift our energy around our shadows.

Yoga nidra works best when guided. I use Insight Timer, which is a free app that offers guided meditations, including plenty of yoga nidra sessions.

Pro tip: Put a stack of pillows or blankets under your knees so your heels dangle. This turns on your parasympathetic nervous system response (see page 111) and helps you go into deeper relaxation more quickly.

Creating the right ritual for you: Your morning practice

Set aside 20 minutes for a healing morning routine. Pick two practices from this chapter or throughout this book, try them out for a week or two, and observe how you feel.

As a new mother at the time of writing this chapter, I've started to get up early to spend 10–20 minutes stretching or doing yoga, then 10–15 minutes meditating or doing breathwork. This time to myself, tending to my body, mind, and spirit, every morning has helped me feel happier and calmer throughout my day.

Other practices to choose from:

☆ Stream of consciousness writing/journaling

☆ Tarot reading

☆ Walking barefoot on grass or sand

☆ Embodiment practice

☆ Making a custom infusion

Tarot Reflections

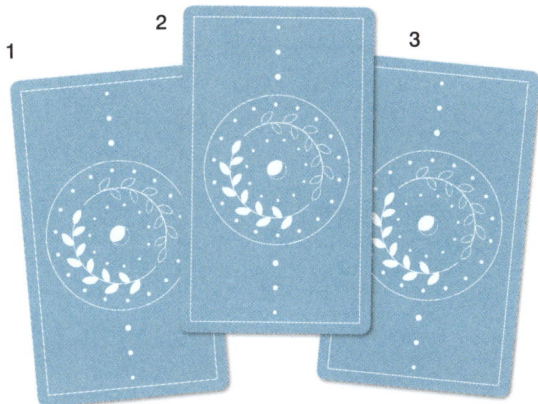

1 2 3

Card 1: Where does energy feel stuck for me right now?

Card 2: What is the root of this blocked energy?

Card 3: How can I move through my healing process with love for myself?

See page 11 for guidance.

Grounding Golden Yellow Lentil Stew with Greens and Garlic Yogurt

Ground down after energy work or a big movement session with a batch of warming, healthy comfort food. The lentils provide plant-based protein, while plenty of anti-inflammatory spices will help soothe the body and spirit. I suggest serving this topped with garlic yogurt, thinly sliced radish, and fresh cilantro/coriander, but I love adding other toppings of whatever I have in the kitchen. Roasted vegetables like sweet potato, butternut squash, or cauliflower are all great in this, and a little hot sauce or more lemon juice can really liven things up.

Serves 6

- ☆ 2 tablespoons grass-fed butter or olive oil
- ☆ 1 yellow onion, peeled and diced
- ☆ 2 stalks celery, finely chopped
- ☆ 1 teaspoon ground coriander
- ☆ 1 teaspoon ground turmeric
- ☆ ½ teaspoon smoked paprika
- ☆ 1lb/450g dried yellow lentils
- ☆ 6 cups/1.4 litres vegetable or chicken broth
- ☆ 1 bunch of kale, destemmed and cut into ribbons or 5oz/140g baby spinach or arugula/rocket
- ☆ zest and juice from ½ lemon
- ☆ radishes, thinly sliced, to serve
- ☆ fresh cilantro/coriander leaves, roughly chopped to serve
- ☆ salt and freshly ground black pepper

Garlic yogurt

- ☆ 1 cup/215g plain Greek yogurt
- ☆ 1 tablespoon olive oil
- ☆ ½ teaspoon garlic powder
- ☆ salt

- ☆ steamed rice to serve (optional)

Heat the butter or olive oil in a large soup pot or dutch oven over a medium heat. Add onion and cook, stirring occasionally, for about 5 minutes until softened and translucent. Add the celery and continue to cook, stirring occasionally, for another 2 minutes.

Stir in the coriander, turmeric, paprika, and a generous pinch of salt and cook for 1 minute. Add the lentils and broth, turn up the heat to medium-high, cover, and bring to a boil. Once boiling, reduce to a simmer over medium-low heat. Cook at a simmer for 20–25 minutes until the lentils are tender and starting to lose their shape a bit.

While lentils are simmering, mix together the ingredients for the garlic yogurt in a small bowl, stirring well until everything is combined and smooth. Set aside or keep in the fridge until you're ready to eat.

Taste the soup for seasoning, adding additional salt and pepper if required. Stir in the greens and cover for about 2 minutes, until wilted. Turn off the heat and stir in the lemon zest and juice.

Serve the lentil stew hot, topped with garlic yogurt, sliced radishes, fresh cilantro/coriander, and rice (if using).

Chapter 9

Manifesting & Honoring Your Shadow

We all have the power to manifest things. I've manifested a few major things in my life—a partner, a cookbook deal, a job. Even though I wasn't consciously manifesting at the time, the ways each of these came into my life were similar.

It started with seeing what I wanted reflected back to me through acquaintances or media. Seeing what was possible gave me both clarity and bolstered my faith that I could have what I wanted. Following intuitive hits was essential to my process, too. Little urges to go places, research things, cut ties with people, and reach out to others, all led me to the right places to receive the things I most wanted. Everyone is able to manifest, we even do it unintentionally or haphazardly, but if we approach it consciously, we can consistently create magic in our lives.

Manifestation is a simple energetic equation, but it can get tripped up when we don't feel deserving of what we want—we only get what we believe we deserve. Feeling unworthy or undeserving usually comes from a deeply rooted shadow. Once we're able to identify and accept our shadow (the parts of ourselves that we try to hide from others), it can actually help us make big things happen.

The idea of shadow and working with it comes from the psychoanalyst Carl Jung, but there are many ways you can do it and interpret it. I've included manifestation and shadow work in the same chapter because I've found that you become far more powerful when you combine the two.

What is Manifestation?

Manifestation is the process of identifying what you want and getting it through a combination of believing that you can have what you're dreaming of, taking action, and showing up as your whole self.

The Law of Attraction

The Law of Attraction (LoA) is a popular principle of manifestation. The general idea is whatever we focus on becomes our reality. If you feel good, good things will come to you. And if you feel bad or view life through a negative lens, you'll continue in a pattern that doesn't serve you. This is the basis of the book *The Secret* by Rhonda Byrne.

The LoA emphasizes the importance of being in a high-vibe state. Followers of Esther and Jerry Hicks/Abraham call this The Vortex. One must be in The Vortex, or feel as if they already have all they want, to call in all the amazing things that they're trying to manifest. And while it's incredibly important to do things every day that make us feel good and put us in a positive and empowered state of mind, I think the Law of Attraction falls short in that it makes us afraid to feel our whole range of feelings and emotions—negative or "bad" ones included.

The LoA has the potential to freak us out into worrying that our negative thoughts will make bad things happen. But we need to allow ourselves to fully feel our emotions to move through them and move on. In fact, negative emotions and feelings can actually help us realize where we might be holding ourselves back.

The LoA does work, but it's essential that we first believe we're worthy of the things we want. Then we can take actions from a place of self-love, not surface-level ego.

Checking your ego is important. If you're trying to manifest for external approval, that's ego desperation. But if you feel intuitively called to manifest something because it will support your sense of security, self-care practice, or self-worth, you're on the right track. You can still manifest the great apartment, dream job, or beautiful wardrobe, but double-check that your motivation is coming from your authentic core self.

Worth-based manifestation

The sad truth is that a lot of us don't feel a deep sense of self-worth or deserving, which is why manifestation remains elusive. We are all born completely worthy beings and following our hearts' desires is what we're meant to do. But society, family dynamics, inherited beliefs, media, teachers, and peers all contribute to distorting our sense of deserving. The process of manifesting and doing shadow work can help shed light on these distortions and restore our core-level sense of worth.

The work of Lacy Phillips, through her website, To Be Magnetic (see page 140) guides you through this worth work with self-hypnosis and journaling tools. Her process is straightforward but deep and combines psychology and neuroscience with intuition and inner work around worthiness and belief.

JUMP IN: **Try Manifesting**

I think of manifestation as an equation: Intention + Self-worth + Acting on intuition + Trust = Manifestation. It seems simple, but consciously manifesting involves putting in the energetic and emotional work to make space for what you want in your life. Here are some helpful steps:

☆ Getting clear on what you want. Get specific (seriously, make a list) and get real—why do you want it?

☆ Believing that you're worthy of what you want

☆ Embracing your shadows

☆ Taking aligned action by following your intuition

☆ Saying no to things that aren't a "hell, yes" and don't make you feel good

☆ Trusting yourself, your power, and the universe

☆ Enjoying the present moment

Being able to be present is a great way of stepping into and owning your power. Presence and enjoyment create a feeling of self-worth and confidence that can help you generate even more of what you want. Manifestation is a continual, non-linear process that we can always be refining, learning from, and making our own.

Finding Freedom Through the Shadow

To feel worthy, we first need to embrace our whole, core self. Getting closer to our core self requires us to look at the parts of ourselves that we're ashamed of, embarrassed by, or have completely denied. This is the shadow. Shadow prevents us from feeling worthy and getting what we want because we believe that these parts of ourselves are so terrible that we'll be rejected if we reveal them.

When we embrace our shadow, we become a more authentic version of ourselves because we're no longer trying to push away or ignore aspects of our whole self. When we're able to own all parts of ourselves, even the things we've deemed bad, we feel worthy because we're no longer at the mercy of what we're hiding. It's a form of freedom.

One of the reasons witches are associated with darkness is because they're willing to face the shadows of themselves to step into their power. Living a more magical life requires us to change the way we've always done things, including the small ways we hide every day. It's not about becoming the shadow, but being okay with it. Shadow work is a way of stripping away conditioning and coming back to our core self. The universe will reward us for that, because that's what we're here to do—be our core self and share our unique powers and gifts with the world.

Identifying your shadow

Being your most authentic self sounds flippant or like something you read on a throw-away Instagram quote, until you start doing shadow work. Working with your shadow isn't easy or fun a lot of the time, but it's crucial to coming back to the core self and healing triggers in order to thrive.

Finding where our shadow lives is easy once we get the hang of it. It shows up in all the ways we feel guilt or shame. It's the things we don't admit to people or try to hide from others because we feel like they won't accept us if we show these parts of ourselves.

Observe yourself as you go through your day and notice what makes you feel ashamed, upset, annoyed, or embarrassed or when you feel like you need something external to cope—like social media, alcohol, or shopping.

LOOSENING THE GRIP

Once we identify our shadow aspects, we need to take the sting out of them. We can do this by meditating, tapping (see page 114), or through self-hypnosis. In her work, Lacy Phillips uses what she calls Deep Imaginings, which are guided meditations or hypnosis sessions (see resources, page 140).

All of these tools seek to bring us to a state of relaxation, from where we can access the subconscious. The goal when we're working with the subconscious is to pinpoint where/when in our lives we may have suppressed our shadows and then help ourselves heal from them.

Because so many of these shadows are formed in early childhood, this can be deep and murky territory. But it's also ripe for inner child work. I often picture my present self comforting a child version of me and giving her what she needs in that moment. It sounds hokey, but this is often the healing that we crave and don't readily give ourselves.

Embracing your shadow

Accepting and even loving our shadowy bits is where we really start to gain power. Think about the most captivating, funny, brilliant, magnetic people you know—I'll bet they openly own their flaws with grace, humor, and honesty.

Owning your sh*t = embracing your shadow. And the more you do it, the more you can start to manifest. There are a few ways you can embrace and own your shadow:

☆ Casually mention it in conversation.

☆ Open up about it to someone close to you.

☆ Do a visualization where this shadow is personified and you physically embrace it or have it become a part of you in a way that feels healing and loving.

Moving through shadow blocks

Your shadow will always find new ways to pop up in your life, which can impede your manifestation. Don't let your shadow block you from creating the life you want, instead find ways to heal your relationship to it. Once you've been triggered by part of your shadow or a deeply rooted belief, you can choose to work with it instead of letting it block you from manifesting. The below techniques can help you work through a sticky shadow issue and release it.

TAPPING OR EFT (EMOTIONAL FREEDOM TECHNIQUE)

Tapping works with the meridian points of the body (like in acupressure or acupuncture) and combines tapping on specific points while saying statements out loud that identify the issue you're dealing with, why you're having problems with it, and what you'd like to change. YouTube is a great resource to learn the basics. For more information on this technique see page 114.

HYPNOSIS OR VISUALIZATION

This is a guided meditation in which you go into a relaxed state with the purpose of diving into the subconscious to help you access the patterns that are holding you back. You can go on a dreamlike journey suited to your purpose (in this case, identifying your block and giving yourself the medicine you need to heal it).

JOURNALING

If you can let your thoughts flow without judgment, the act of taking pen to paper can be healing for both unlocking something you may have closed off and finding a way forward.

BREATHWORK

Focused breathing that works with the spiritual, emotional, and physical body. It hits on many of the energy centers and can help move stagnant energy, often bringing emotions, inherited beliefs, and pain up and out. For more information on this technique see page 113.

Know that you have the power to change. Just knowing that you hold this capability can help you approach those triggers that are keeping you small and reductive with confidence and curiosity.

Cultivating your Worthiness

Showing up as your core self in every situation is the ultimate display of healthy self-worth. It feels like a resounding, "I'm just going to do me." It's feeling into that freedom of being yourself and not caring what others think of it. No one is perfect at this, but our work is to continually practice coming into alignment with our core self.

Self-worth practices

Feeling into and bolstering our self-worth takes dedication and practice, especially because our brains are wired to make us doubt the greatness that is our core self. Here are a few ways to give that self-worth an extra boost. Do these in tandem with shadow work for best manifesting results.

GRATITUDE PRACTICE

Can you focus on what you have at the moment instead of looking to get more? Gratitude practice is about being present with what is and appreciating it. Having gratitude for things you've already cultivated in your life can give you real, tangible examples of your power and worth.

Try to record your gratitudes daily or weekly for the best results. List 5 or 10 things, or set a timer for 5 minutes and get out as much as you can. You can do it by journaling them (see page 131), making voice memos for yourself or sending them to a friend, or sending them in a text message to a friend.

CARING FOR YOURSELF

Self-care is a reflection of self-worth. Set aside some time each day or a couple of times a week to do something for yourself that feels good. This doesn't have to be anything fancy or elaborate, as long as it feels restorative. This can look like napping, cooking for yourself, watching a movie on the couch, alone time, a walk outside, listening to a podcast, meditating, or buying yourself tea and chocolate.

Write out a self-care menu of all the things that make you feel good. Anything that makes you feel warm and cozy, relaxed, restored, energized, or supported—put it all down on a list that you can refer to when you're feeling a little low or lacking energy. Then commit to doing one of these things regularly. By following through on caring for yourself, you communicate your worth to yourself and the universe.

CLEARING

We need to make space for new things to come into our lives. If it's not lighting you up, start saying no. You don't have to take on projects you hate, deal with people who make you feel bad, or keep doing something just because you're scared that something better won't come along. Start believing in the power of saying no to clear away things that don't feel good to you. Clearing can mean physically clearing clutter that's dragging you down, or changing the way you approach something—for example, deciding to only check your inbox once a day. It can also bring up bigger things like reassessing your job or relationships and setting up boundaries.

Look at each area of your life and think about what feels good and what feels less than good, and begin making adjustments by saying no or outsourcing what you can. Start small and begin to see the changes that take hold.

Getting into Alignment

Alignment is when you're moving through the world with your core self leading the way. When you do this, you're able to follow your intuition and get into a state of flow. Alignment is kind of like all the parts working together—knowing your worth, embracing your whole self, feeling good, and having clarity. If we can operate from a place of alignment, we're able to manifest more easily.

Whether you're at your desk working or visiting a new place, being in this aligned flow has a few tell-tale signs:
1. You feel good. You're energized, calm, and positive.
2. Things come naturally. Whether it's what to write, who to reach out to, where to go, or what to do next, there is a secure feeling of just knowing and doing it. Nothing feels forced, it just feels right.
3. More good things flow. Flow creates more flow and if you're acting in alignment, things will keep coming in—including what you're manifesting.

Not every day will or can feel like a magical aligned experience, and often things rock us out of that feeling of flow—a challenging commute, your bank balance, other people's bad energy. It's important not to let these things get you down too much (easier said than done, I know) and try to come back to that core part of yourself. One thing that I find helpful to remember is that you can also choose to be in alignment, which is really where your power lies.

It can often feel like alignment is elusive and the conditions must be just right in order to get into that zone. But that's not true, sometimes you just need to change your energy and your alignment will shift.

Change your energy

Try any of the following:

★ Moving for 5 minutes. Dancing is a great way to do this. So is orgasming, doing hip circles, jumping up and down, doing a downward dog, or taking a walk around the block.

★ Sitting, breathing, and meditating with the intention of coming back to your core self.

★ Putting on some music or changing the music that's playing.

★ Clearing out all distractions and setting a timer for 30 minutes to focus on one task. Setting a small time frame takes the pressure off.

★ Gratitude practice (see page 132).

★ Going somewhere new. Work from a cafe instead of at home, get lunch somewhere new, take a walk down a street you normally don't. Seeing things with fresh eyes can spark the intuition.

★ Stream of consciousness writing.

★ Pulling a Tarot card or two (see Chapter 6).

★ Resetting by eating a nourishing meal.

Creating the right ritual for you: Casting a spell

Writing down what you'd like to manifest is a powerful act. It solidifies your desires within your brain and in the universe, initiating magic. Spells are intentions that are specifically spoken, felt, and put out into the world. The most important aspects are your intention and feeling it in your body. If a spell doesn't feel right to you, it might not do much, so creating your own spells based on your intuition and preferences is a great practice.

Spell formula

1. Set an intention. What do you want? Are you calling something in? Releasing something? Setting a boundary?
2. Craft the words. Write out your intention along with any other language you want to include, like calling on your guides and the universe along with a couple of other strong sentences.

3. Add tools. Choose candles, plants, essential oils, incense, artwork, food, crystals—whatever feels aligned.
4. Put it all together. Set up your tools on an altar or cleared space and say the words you prepared out loud. Repeat them if it feels right.
5. Seal your spell with a simple act of self-care, like drinking a glass of water or an infusion, having a piece of chocolate, or taking a shower.

Tarot Reflections

  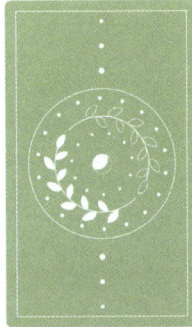

Card 1: What part of my core self wants to be seen and loved right now?

Card 2: How can I deepen my sense of self-worth?

Card 3: What will aid me in my manifestation process today?

See page 11 for guidance.

Walnut Pesto and Brain-Health Bowl

As we're reworking our relationship to our shadow and beliefs around self-worth and personal power, we'll need plenty of brain support. The thinking mind loves patterns, so it puts up a fight when we try to change the way we think—because it's easier and more energy-efficient to stick to the patterns we've built up over time. Be gentle with yourself and give your head a little extra love and attention with brain-healthy foods, which this bowl and pesto are packed with. Walnuts, greens, blueberries, tomatoes, eggs, avocado, and whole grains are all incredible brain food.

You can also use the pesto on pasta, eggs, sandwiches, etc. You can also substitute basil for half basil half parsley, all parsley, or all cilantro/coriander.

Makes ½ cup/100g pesto

Walnut Pesto

* ½ cup/50g raw walnut halves or pieces
* 1 bunch of basil (about 2 cups/40g)
* freshly squeezed juice of ½ lemon
* 1 tablespoon nutritional yeast
* ½ garlic clove
* 1 teaspoon white miso paste
* ½ cup/120ml extra virgin olive oil
* salt

Makes 1 bowl

Brain-Health Bowl

* 2 cups/100g kale, cleaned and finely sliced into ribbons
* ½ cup/60g cooked wild rice or other whole grain (cooked weight)
* 1 soft-boiled egg, cut in half
* ½ avocado, cut into chunks
* ⅓ cup/60g grape/small plum tomatoes, halved
* ½ cup/60g blueberries
* 2 tablespoons pepitas/pumpkin seeds, toasted

Preheat the oven to 350°F/175°C/Gas 4.

To make the pesto, spread the raw walnuts on a baking tray and place in the preheated oven for 7–9 minutes, until lightly toasted and fragrant. Set aside to cool. When the walnuts have cooled, place in a food processor or blender with all the remaining pesto ingredients and purée until smooth and everything is finely chopped and well combined.

Combine the kale in a mixing bowl with 2 spoonfuls of pesto and a pinch of salt. Massage the pesto into the kale with your hands for about 30 seconds until the kale starts to soften. Add the cooked rice to the kale and toss to combine.

Place the pesto kale and rice in your serving bowl and top with the rest of the bowl ingredients. Serve with more pesto if desired.

Helpful reminders

Creating a magical life is an ongoing process. It takes time and resilience to make significant changes and we need to find ways to bolster ourselves as we go. Please know that you're not alone in wanting to feel abundant, peaceful, free, wild, strong, soft, and magic all at once. Consider this your official welcome to the coven of individuals who take charge of their own lives and change for the better.

Before I go, I'd like to leave you with a few things I often have to remind myself of along this path of healing and transformation. These are a mix of personal aphorisms and intentions to which I continually come back to reassure and steady myself in moments when I'm met with resistance. I hope they can serve as loving reminders to you, too.

Go slower.

Trust, nurture, and show up for yourself.

Let go.

Give yourself the gift of time and space.

Breathe.

Follow the sparks that light you up.

Find pleasure in the everyday.

Crack your heart open.

Move through the world with tenderness.

Trust there is always enough.

Your body is your ally.

Taking care of yourself first will help you show up fully for others.

You have the answers you seek.

Resources

Chapter 1: Embracing the Feminine

EMBODIMENT

Alexandra Roxo
alexandraroxo.com

5 Rhythms
5rhythms.com

CYCLE SYNCING

WomanCode by Alisa Vitti,
HarperOne, 2013

FEMALE SEXUALITY AND SEXUAL HEALTH

OMG Yes
omgyes.com

O School
www.o.school

Chapter 2: Mirroring Nature & the Seasons

Lindsay Mack of Wild Soul Healing
lindsaymack.com

BOOKS

Witch: Unleashed, Untamed, Unapologetic by Lisa Lister,
Hay House, 2017

Chapter 3: Creating a Magical Home

Cunningham's Encyclopedia of Magical Herbs by Scott Cunningham,
Llewellyn Publications, 1985

The House Witch by Arin Murphy-Hiscock, Adams Media, 2018

Energy Muse
energymuse.com

Mountain Rose Herbs
mountainroseherbs.com

Chapter 4: Lunar Living

Lunar Abundance by Ezzie Spencer,
Running Press, 2018

Moon Journal by Sandy Sitron,
Chronicle Books, 2018

Radical Awakenings
alexandraroxo.mykajabi.com/
community

Mystic Mamma
mysticmamma.com

APPS

Moon Phase Calendar Plus
apps.apple.com/us/app/moon-phase-calendar-plus/id671352640

TimePassages Astrology
apps.apple.com/us/app/
timepassages-astrology/id488946918

Chapter 5: Self-Awareness with Astrology

Alchemy with Ambi
alchemywithambi.com

Cacao Laboratory
cacaolaboratory.com

Danielle Beinstein
daniellebeinstein.com

Bess Matassa
thestarparlor.com

Mystic Medusa
mysticmedusa.com

CHANI
chani.com/today/current-sky

Sandy Sitron
sandysitron.com

The Strology
thestrology.com

APPS

Time Passages Astrology
apps.apple.com/us/app/
timepassages-astrology/id488946918

Sanctuary Psychic Reading
apps.apple.com/us/app/sanctuary-psychic-reading/id1417411962

Co–Star
costarastrology.com

BOOKS

The Stars Within You by Juliana
McCarthy, Roost Books, 2018

The Only Astrology Book You'll Ever Need by Joanna Martine, Woolfolk
Taylor Trade Publishing, 2012

Chapter 6: Connect to Your Wisdom with Tarot

Lindsay Mack of Wild Soul Healing
lindsaymack.com

Anna Toonk
annatoonk.com

Biddy Tarot
biddytarot.com

Tatianna Tarot
@tatiannatarot on Instagram

Brandon Alter
@thebrandonalter on Instagram

Tarot Bytes: The Podcast
with Theresa Reed
thetarotlady.com/tarot-bytes

The Moonchild Tarot
daniellenoel.art/pages/moonchild

The Wild Unknown Tarot
kimkrans.com/the-wild-unknown

BOOKS

78 Degrees of Wisdom by Rachel Pollack, First Edition: Aquarian Books, 1980; Weiser Books, 2007 and 2019

WTF is Tarot? And How Do I Do It? by Bakara Wittner, Page Street Publishing, 2017

Modern Tarot by Michele Tea, HarperOne, 2017

Chapter 7: Herbs & Plant Medicine for Wellbeing

Herbal Academy
theherbalacademy.com

Memorial Sloan Kettering Cancer Center: The Integrative Medicine Herb Search
mskcc.org/cancer-care/diagnosis-treatment/symptom-management/integrative-medicine/herbs/search

BOOKS

Cunningham's Encyclopedia of Magical Herbs by Scott Cunningham, Llewellyn Publications, 1985

Alchemy of Herbs by Rosalee de la Foret, Hay House, 2017

Herbal Healing for Women by Rosemary Gladstar, Atria Books, 1993

BUYING HERBS

Mountain Rose Herbs
www.mountainroseherbs.com

FLOWER ESSENCES

Alexis Smart Flower Remedies
alexissmart.com

Deer Heart Apothecary
deerheartapothecary.com/

Original Bach Flower Remedies
bachflower.com

CBD BRANDS

MINERAL
mineralhealth.co

Rosebud
rosebudcbd.com

Charlotte's Web
charlottesweb.com

Lord Jones
lordjones.ca

Chapter 8: Healing with Energy Flow & Movement

MOVEMENT

Yoga with Adriene
youtube.com/@yogawithadriene

5 Rhythms
5rhythms.com

intenSati
intensati.com

REIKI

The International Center for Reiki Training
reiki.org

Self-Healing with Reiki by Penelope Quest, TarcherPerigee, 2012

BREATHWORK TEACHERS

Erin Telford
erintelford.com

David Elliot
davidelliott.com

Amy Kuretsky
amykuretsky.com

BOOKS

How to Breathe by Ashley Neese, Ten Speed Press, 2019

Healing by David Elliott, Hawk Press, 2010

TAPPING/EFT

The Tapping Solution Foundation
tappingsolutionfoundation.org

Gala Darling
youtube.com/@galadarling

APP

Insight Timer
apps.apple.com/us/app/insight-timer-meditate-sleep/id337472899

Chapter 9: Manifesting & Honoring your Shadow

To Be Magnetic by Lacy Phillips
tobemagnetic.com

The Holistic Psychologist
yourholisticpsychologist.com

Ziva Meditation
zivameditation.com

BOOKS

Meeting the Shadow: The Hidden Power of the Dark Side of Human Nature by Connie Zweig and Jeremiah Abrams, TarcherPerigee, 1991

The Power of Vulnerability by Brene Brown, Sounds True, 2012

Close Your Eyes, Get Free: Use Self-Hypnosis to Reduce Stress, Quit Bad Habits, and Achieve Greater Relaxation and Focus by Grace Smith, Da Capo Lifelong Books, 2018

Index

Acknowledgments

Writing this book was one of the more challenging projects I've taken on. A shift in focus and a pregnancy brought changes at every level of my work and life, and at times I thought I didn't deserve to be writing about these topics. This book wouldn't have been possible without a great team supporting me.

I'd like to thank my editors Kristine Pidkameny and Dawn Bates for your attention and care. My agent Sharon Bowers for getting behind me on this idea and Cindy Richards for agreeing to bring it to life. Many thanks to the design team at CICO Books, especially Sally Powell and Eliana Holder. I know I'm annoyingly particular and you both worked very hard to make this book beautiful. And thanks to Belle Daughtry for your gorgeous photography.

Thank you to my teachers, who appear throughout these pages and have contributed to my expanding knowledge and continual healing. From my first breathwork circle with Jordan Catherine Pagán, to Tarot Sundays at Maha Rose with Anna Toonk, to monthly check-ins with Alexandra Roxo and Moon Club, to the astrological insights of Sandy Sitron and Shakirah Tabourn.

To all my pizza witches who let me read their cards as a newbie and asked their moms for their birth times, thank you for letting me insist on things being #covengoals.

And Fabian. Thank you for always being my biggest supporter, the best Dad to Maeve and partner I could ever wish for. Our life together is bigger and better than anything I could put on a manifestation list.

And last, but not (at all) least, thank you reader, for picking up this book. Even though, I'm still on my healing journey and am learning more every day, I'm filled with so much gratitude for being able to write this book at this time in my life.

xoLeah

Picture credits

Photography by **Belle Daughtry**, except for the following:

Clare Winfield/Ryland, Peters & Small: p123

David Merewether: p15

Gary Crabbe / Enlightened Images / Alamy Stock Photo: pp 54–55

Leah Vanderveldt: pp 3, 8, 35, 36, 39, 40, 53, 67, 93, 137

Nuclear_xonix/Adobe Stock: pp 68–69

Tarot cards are from *The Art of Tarot* by Liz Dean, published by CICO Books